CONTENTS

U.S.-UK RELATIONS AT THE START OF THE 21st CENTURY

Edited by

**Jeffrey D. McCausland
Douglas T. Stuart**

January 2006

*****

The views expressed in this volume are those of the authors and do not necessarily reflect the official policy or position of the Department of the Army, the Department of Defense, or the U.S. Government. This report is cleared for public release; distribution is unlimited.

*****

Michael Calingaert wishes to thank Leo Buzzerio and Andrew Felton for their assistance in the preparation of Chapter 2, "The Special Relationship: Economic/Business."

*****

Comments pertaining to this report are invited and should be forwarded to: Director, Strategic Studies Institute, U.S. Army War College, 122 Forbes Ave, Carlisle, PA 17013-5244.

*****

All Strategic Studies Institute (SSI) monographs are available on the SSI Homepage for electronic dissemination. Hard copies of this report also may be ordered from our Homepage. SSI's Homepage address is: *www.StrategicStudiesInstitute.army.mil./*

*****

The Strategic Studies Institute publishes a monthly e-mail newsletter to update the national security community on the research of our analysts, recent and forthcoming publications, and upcoming conferences sponsored by the Institute. Each newsletter also provides a strategic commentary by one of our research analysts. If you are interested in receiving this newsletter, please subscribe on our homepage at *www. StrategicStudiesInstitute.army.mil/ssi/newsletter/.*

ISBN 1-58487-217-9

INTRODUCTION

With the end of the Cold War, a popular parlor game in foreign ministries, think tanks, and academia has been to develop a theory of international relations that best explains the new international order. Although there is widespread agreement that the United States is the world's most powerful country in military, economic, and diplomatic terms, and is likely to remain so for the foreseeable future, there is little agreement as to how the rest of the world will react to America's lead. Concepts such as "balancing," "bandwagoning," "buck-passing," and "free riding," to name just a few, have been advanced and debated. And although none presents a unified field theory, each explains some aspect of international relations.

Theory has an even more difficult time explaining the relationship between the United States and the United Kingdom (UK), especially its remarkable endurance over the past 6 decades. The U.S.-UK partnership flourished during World War II, deepened during the long twilight struggle with the Soviet Union, and has prospered further since the end of the Cold War. It is likely to survive any new challenges that may loom on the horizon.

The United States has the same track record with no other state, even those who were also once part of the British Empire. America's relations with Canada, our neighbor and largest trading partner, and with Australia, with whom we share a common heritage of mass immigration and frontier-taming, are robust, yet do not attain quite the same scope and depth as the U.S.-UK special relationship.

Many observers and commentators, even former officials who should know better, ascribe the success of the relationship to an affinity of purpose, rooted in a shared heritage of law, traditions, blood ties, and culture. They have a tendency to place the relationship on a pedestal, to be handled reverently as if by liveried servants. They conjure up endless vistas of Anglo-American harmony, unblemished by harsh words or furrowed brows—vistas of sunny days and clear skies, of unanimity on all matters, large and small.

Nothing could be further from the truth. An accurate history, not hagiography, is essential to understanding the relationship and what makes it special. Our interests are similar, but not always identical. Our strategic goals may overlap, but our tactics may differ.

Almost from its inception, the relationship has been fraught with disagreement and acrimony, often over existential matters of war and peace. No sooner had our extensive wartime collaboration succeeded in defeating the Axis powers than Washington passed the Atomic Energy Act of 1946, which terminated all atomic energy cooperation with the UK. Quickly forgotten was the immense contribution British scientists had made to the Manhattan Project. Less than a decade later, Washington and London had a fundamental and very public disagreement over Suez, with the United States eventually compelling the removal of all British forces from Egypt by forcing a sterling crisis that threatened to bankrupt the UK. These were two of the earliest, and in some ways the most startling, of a series of disagreements the two countries have had, and continue to have, on issues that affect their interests and the world. More recently, the United States and the UK have worked closely together to advance the peace process in Northern Ireland. But it hasn't always been smooth sailing.

During the 1960s and 1970s, American politicians like Hugh Carey, Daniel Patrick Moynihan, Thomas Phillip "Tip" O'Neill, Jr., and Edward "Ted" Kennedy were among the first to draw international attention to the discrimination against the Catholic community in education, employment, and housing in Northern Ireland. The Clinton administration weathered a firestorm with the British over its decision to grant a visa to Gerry Adams, entertain him at the White House, and generally elevate the profile of Sinn Fein. On Northern Ireland, there have been other disagreements over the years, although no one doubts the fundamental commitment of all American administrations, and especially President Bush, to the peace process.

It is in these disagreements that the true nature of the special relationship can be found. It is our ability to disagree, to argue passionately, candidly, and forcefully with each other — and then to pick up the pieces, place our anger behind us, and go forward together—that makes the relationship special and explains why it has thrived. Disagreement *and* resolution are the hallmark signs of a healthy partnership. Despite being a cliché, it nonetheless is true that the United States has no more reliable, trustworthy, or stalwart ally than the United Kingdom. I believe the UK feels the same way about the United States.

So how best to explain this special relationship? It may simply defy categorization. Like the theater owner in the film *Shakespeare in Love* (another Anglo-American collaboration) explaining how plays are produced, "It's a mystery." But it is very special nonetheless.

AMBASSADOR MITCHELL B. REISS
Special Envoy to the Northern Ireland Peace Process
Washington, DC

ACKNOWLEDGMENTS

In reality, this project has its roots in our collective experiences for over 30 years. We have both had the good fortune to work, think, debate, discuss, and reflect on issues affecting international security in general, and transatlantic relations in particular, throughout our professional careers. In the process, we were fortunate to meet and get to know a tremendous group of British colleagues, due to the very close relationship our country and the United Kingdom (UK) shared during the Cold War. Following the collapse of the Soviet Union and the horrific events of September 11, 2001, it seemed only appropriate to undertake an in-depth audit of this unique relationship. We are both, therefore, indebted to a host of friends and mentors with whom we have worked over the years on various aspects of British-American relations and on common problems facing both our countries.

This book is a compilation of all of the papers submitted during the conferences we conducted at both Dickinson College and the Defense Academy of the United Kingdom on the topic "The Future of the Special Relationship." We are grateful to the outstanding group of experts who contributed their collective wisdom to our discussions and this volume. This effort also reflects the hard work and assistance of a number of other people. First, we wish to thank the Strategic Studies Institute (SSI), the Center for Strategic and International Studies (CSIS), and the Royal United Services Institute (RUSI) for their support and guidance, and for hosting events associated with this project. We are also extremely grateful for the assistance which we received from Mr. Tom Kalaris, CEO, Americas, for Barclays Capital, and a Trustee of Dickinson College. We are also very proud of four Dickinson students—Sara Lybeck, Alex Stout, Helena Berrizbeitia, and Dan Emery—for their superb contributions to the conferences' overall success. In the UK, we were warmly hosted by the Advanced Research and Analysis Group (ARAG) at the Defense Academy of the United Kingdom. We wish to express our thanks to Christopher Donnelly, ARAG Director, and Sara Auchinleck, Research Manager. Finally, we are both particularly indebted to the staff of the Leadership in Conflict Initiative, Kitzi Chappelle and Tanya McCausland, for their tireless efforts in organizing and arranging the conferences associated with this volume. Without them this effort would never have succeeded.

JEFFREY D. McCAUSLAND, Director
Leadership in Conflict Initiative,
Department of International Studies,
Dickinson College

DOUGLAS T. STUART
Professor of Political Science
and International Studies
Dickinson College

CHAPTER 1

THE U.S.-UK SPECIAL RELATIONSHIP IN HISTORICAL CONTEXT: LESSONS OF THE PAST

Ray Raymond

Winston Churchill once wrote, "Learn all you can from history, for how else can one even make a guess what is going to happen in the future . . . in history lie all the secrets of statecraft." Churchill was right, and his advice is especially appropriate to the study of the special relationship. Properly understood, the lessons of the past not only help us keep the problems of the present in perspective, but also point to one central conclusion: some kind of intimate and unbreakable link does exist between the United States and Britain, and its roots are very deep.

Throughout the deliberations of the two conferences that form the basis of this book, I was struck that so many of my fellow participants knew so little of the history of the Anglo-American relationship. Stereotypes abounded, particularly in the British delegation. Many of these participants appeared eager to deny the existence of a shared heritage so critical in helping us resolve disputes past and present. This chapter attempts to explain what the special relationship is and to provide a more balanced view of its value.

KEEPING THE PRESENT IN PERSPECTIVE

To begin, the lessons of the past put our current problems in perspective. Anti-Americanism is one example. Throughout the Carlisle and Shrivenham conferences, many participants expressed serious concern about the extent, intensity, and nature of anti-Americanism in the United Kingdom. They were right to do so. The current level of anti-Americanism is indeed disturbing and, in my judgment, poses the biggest single threat to the special relationship. But anti-Americanism in Britain is nothing new. It has been a prominent feature of the ideology of the left and right wings of British politics ever since 1945. Yet, over the past 60 years, the special relationship has not only survived but prospered, making a vital contribution to international security.

The years immediately following World War II offer a very good example. The war had marked a substantial shift in economic power — and hence political and military power — from Britain to the United States. This was a terrible shock to a proud nation accustomed to controlling the destiny of much of the world. The psychological repercussions of this transfer of power were clearly identifiable in a strongly anti-American mood intensified by moral unease over the dropping of the atomic bombs on Japan, resentment at the abrupt termination of Lend Lease, and fear that the rapid demobilization and withdrawal of U.S. forces from Europe would leave a weakened Britain unable to deter Soviet aggression. In August 1948, U.S. Ambassador Lew Douglas reported to Washington that "there is an undercurrent of feeling here against the U.S., both in and out of government . . . at times their attitude towards the U.S. borders on the pathological." But this intense anti-Americanism did not prevent Britain and the United States from collaborating closely to ensure the success of the Marshall Plan in 1947, nor did it impede the Anglo-American diplomacy that led to the foundation of the North Atlantic Treaty Organization (NATO) in 1949.

History also reminds us that vigorous arguments between London and Washington are nothing new. There was never a golden age of Anglo-American relations free from acrimony. Franklin D. Roosevelt and Churchill had profound disagreements on the desirability of the continuation of the British Empire in Africa, Asia, and the Middle East, and of the continued existence of British imperial trade preferences in the postwar era. These disagreements were compounded by difficulties over the detailed arrangements for Lend Lease, over British sterling and dollar balances, and over access by U.S. companies to protected markets within the Empire and Commonwealth. On military strategy and tactics, Churchill — the incorrigible worshiper of the periphery — had ferocious arguments with Dwight Eisenhower and George Marshall, who remained wedded to a cross-channel attack on the core of Nazi power.

The true essence of the special relationship was captured in a lunchtime conversation in Washington in the late 1980s when Lord Franks, who had been British Ambassador during the Harry Truman administration, asked the then current Ambassador Sir Oliver Wright, "How are things?" Sir Oliver replied, "Oh, just fine. I have got about six rows going on with the administration and Congress at present." Lord Franks replied, "Oh, good . . . sounds normal to me." The point is that, over the decades, there have been frequent strong disagreements between London and Washington, but they have never prevented us from working effectively together to achieve shared objectives so long as the disagreements were conducted in private like family squabbles. Picking fights in public with the United States is utterly counterproductive.

History also shows that the other grave threat to the special relationship is the continued miniaturization of the British armed forces. As Lord Renwick, one of our greatest Ambassadors in Washington, has shrewdly observed: "Britain has influence on American policy to the extent that it still has some power and influence itself in various parts of the world . . . the price of consultation is presence and participation." In other words, sound, unvarnished advice and diplomatic support—though welcome—will not be enough. The more and the more relevant military capability we have, the greater will be our influence in Washington. The reduction of the British armed forces must stop.

THE LONG-TERM ROOTS OF THE SPECIAL RELATIONSHIP

Some years ago, the elder President George Bush described the special relationship as "the rock upon which all dictators this century have perished." He was referring to the importance of the special relationship in combating fascism and communism in the 20th century. In the 21st century, the special relationship has confounded the skeptics by emerging with renewed vigor. President George W. Bush, for example, frequently describes Britain as America's most important global ally in the war on terror. British Prime Minister Tony Blair commands the stage in Washington and the admiration of the American public as no other British leader since Churchill.

Among the cynical British chattering classes, it has long been fashionable to dismiss the special relationship as mere "rhetorical nonsense, sometimes majestic and often moving, yet nevertheless nonsense." And yet even the most hardened cynics have been forced to admit that some kind of intimate connection does exist between the United States and Britain. But defining it is not easy. The special relationship is not like a sentence that you can parse or a treaty that you can analyze. The most intriguing clue I have found is in a speech given in London by John Hay in the early 1890s when he was U.S. Ambassador to the Court of St. James. Describing the Anglo-American relationship, John Hay said that Britain and the United States "are bound by a tie we did not forge and which we cannot break; we are joint ministers of the same sacred mission of liberty." Hay's insightful phrase suggests to me that to unravel the mystery of the special relationship we need a longer historical perspective; that we need to understand the American Revolution in its full complexity as well as the three pillars of the relationship—the shared common law heritage, the mutual economic investments, and the diplomatic and security ties.

What I am suggesting, contrary to conventional wisdom, is that this relationship does have the "patina of antiquity," and that the usual view of Anglo-American relations—warm and close since 1941, cold and distant before—is mistaken. Instead, I want to offer a provocative working hypothesis: that the solution to the mystery, the real reason the special relationship is special, is that so much of the basic DNA of the infrastructure of the American political, legal, and economic system is British. And I will go further: the basic assumption of Roosevelt's security policy in World War II—the idea that the United States and Britain shared a common strategic interest in preventing a single hostile power from dominating the European continent—can be traced back to the Federalists' foreign policy of the 1790s. In a very real sense, therefore, the United States, however foreign it may sometimes appear to many modern-day Britons, is—to borrow David Hacket Fisher's memorable phrase—"Albion's seed."

Therefore, let's linger a moment on the American Revolution, a subject on which the latest British and American scholarship offers some fascinating insights. To begin with, this scholarship suggests that the secession of the American colonies and the birth of the American Republic were not inevitable. Until well into the 1770s, whatever differences the colonies may have had with London or with each other, few questioned their common allegiance to the crown or their intense pride in their common British identity. Some—including the illustrious Benjamin Franklin—thought the center of gravity of the

4

British Empire and perhaps even its capital eventually must shift to the United States.

The Founders of the British Empire in America envisaged a loose maritime commercial empire cemented by the 17th-century Puritan concept of liberty which was rooted in resistance to the idea of an Absolutist Monarch. This concept of liberty meant parliamentary consent to taxation, representative government, habeas corpus, trial by jury, and protection of the individual citizen from arbitrary arrest and from a corrupt government. As Simon Schama has written, this concept of liberty also included,

> the constant reiteration of its historical epics — Magna Carta, the Petition of Right, and most recently, and therefore most hallowed, the Bill of Rights of 1689 and its heroes and martyrs: John Hampden, John Milton, and Algernon Sidney (ironically, the same heroes and martyrs beloved by John Adams, Thomas Jefferson, and Benjamin Franklin) . . . . The British Empire was supposed to satisfy itself with just enough power, and just enough regulation, to make the interlocking parts of its economic machinery work with well-oiled smoothness.

Those American colonists who had taken these professions of freedom seriously felt betrayed. In the end, they rebelled not because of excessive taxation — the was merely a convenient rallying cry — but because they were concerned that the most sacred principles of British freedom were at stake; that they were the custodians of the true British Constitution which had been abandoned by a corrupt oligarchy in London. I believe they were right. The government of Lord North, in order to protect short-term economic interests, abandoned Pitt the Elder's concept of an empire of liberty based on mutual consent and respect. It was a disastrous mistake. The underlying issue was one of constitutional principle: the difficulty was the failure of the British government to adhere to its own professed ideals of liberty, coupled with the failure of both the American colonists and the British government to agree to a constitutional relationship that clearly defined the rights of the colonial assemblies and the authority of the Westminster Parliament. The American War of Independence, therefore, can be seen as a legitimate rebellion rooted in the English common law. The colonists were not trying to reject their treasured British heritage, but rather to reaffirm and reclaim it from a foolish King and a corrupt political cadre.

The American War of Independence can also be seen as a tragic British civil war in that it divided social classes, towns, villages, and families both in Britain and in the 13 colonies. At least one-third of the colonists—including Benjamin Franklin's son and John Jay's brother—remained loyal to the crown. In Britain, large numbers of Puritans and other religious dissenters strongly supported the American cause because of a shared religion, shared values, and a heartfelt community of friendship. They were joined by English republicans and other radicals whose grandparents had supported Cromwell and the Parliamentary cause against the Stuart Kings: the skilled craftsmen, shopkeepers, and owners of taverns and coffee houses in London, in East Anglia, and in the industrial towns of central England. Opposition to the war also included many elements of the press, as well as members of the Whig opposition in the House of Commons and Lords and many senior officers in the British army and Royal Navy who were especially reluctant to take up arms against their kith and kin in America. This was not, therefore, the case of a united American nation fighting British imperialists determined to subjugate it by force, but rather of one transatlantic "Anglosphere" divided against itself.

Pillar I: Common Law.

The first pillar of the special relationship is, of course, the shared heritage that was and is our great common law tradition. The central point here is that America's Founding Fathers enthusiastically embraced the profoundly British concept of a law-based state shaped by centuries of British political philosophy, jurisprudence, and practice dating back to the Magna Carta. As a result, our shared conception of individual freedom, of a law-based state, and of the pragmatic common law approach to justice rooted in custom, experience, and precedent is now firmly embedded in the American legal system. America's founding documents—the Declaration of Independence, the U.S. Constitution, and the Bill of Rights—do not divide us. They unite us. As Winston Churchill once said, "The Declaration of Independence and the U.S. Constitution are not only American documents. They follow on the Magna Carta and the English Bill of Rights as the great title deeds in which the liberties of the English-speaking peoples are founded." As leading colonial American historians have demonstrated, this was not mere Churchillian romanticism, fuelled by several after-dinner brandies. The political and legal structures created by the colonists were deeply rooted in British constitutional history, political philosophy, and jurisprudence

In its form and content, the Declaration of Independence, for example, is a profoundly British document and part of a centuries-old British tradition. Pauline Maier has shown that, in both England and Scotland, declarations were important political and legal instruments. Politically, declarations were issued to explain and justify the removal of a king. For the Founding Fathers, the most important declaration was the English Declaration of Rights of 1689. It ended the reign of King James II and began that of William and Mary. For the Founding Fathers, the English Declaration became a key source of inspiration: a document which set out certain fundamental political and legal truths to inspire and shape the political and legal structures of the new American republic, as well as to proclaim the end of an old regime.

Jefferson used the English Declaration of Rights as his model when writing the preamble of his constitution for Virginia, one of the two texts we know he had with him in his lodgings in Philadelphia that hot summer of 1776. The other was George Mason's Declaration of Rights for Virginia which was even more closely modeled on the English Declaration of Rights. So Jefferson, the assiduous student of British law and history, was acting as so many Britons had acted before him: drawing up a declaration to explain and justify bringing the reign of George III to an end in his American colonies.

And it is not just a matter of form, but of content. Jefferson relied heavily on two of the leading thinkers of the 18th-century Scottish Enlightenment—David Hume and Francis Hutcheson—for many of his ideas. Hutcheson, for example, wrote that human rights included the right of a people to oppose tyranny and the right of colonies to secede if their mother country treated them unjustly. English philosopher John Locke argued that sovereignty derived from the people, who have a right to remove an unjust monarch. This argument clearly shaped Jefferson's thinking. Indeed, much of the language in the opening paragraphs of the Declaration of Independence closely resembles passages from Locke's Two Treatises of Government. As Dick Howard has written, the English Bill of Rights not only "anticipates the American document of a century later, but also some of the American bill's specific provisions—for example, the Eighth Amendment's ban on excessive bail and fines and on cruel and unusual punishment."

That leads me to a central point as best expressed by the distinguished colonial American historian Gordon Wood:

> The English had worked out a respect for the law and a semblance of popular self-government, however flawed by modern standards, long before the Americans. Whatever innovations Americans made to their English heritage, and they were undeniably considerable, their ultimate success in governing themselves and protecting individual freedom owed more to their English heritage than in did to their constitutional inventions in 1787. From decades of experience they had acquired an instinctive knowledge of English liberty and the English Common Law, and this inherited and inherent knowledge, this long experience with English political culture, was what ultimately enabled them to succeed as well as they did in establishing new governments.

Pillar II: Mutual Investment.

The second pillar of the Anglo-American relationship is the extraordinary interpenetration of our two economies. Today, Britain and America invest over $250 billion in each other's economies, more than any two other countries, and they lead in cross-border mergers and acquisitions. This relationship did not begin yesterday. For over 300 years, the prosperity of Britain and America has always been closely linked. Indeed, the great paradox of the American Revolution is that those rebelling against the Crown in the 1770s were its wealthiest subjects, to a large degree the beneficiaries of British investment and trade.

The foundation of the modern investment relationship can be traced to Alexander Hamilton's tenure as the first U.S. Treasury Secretary. The American War of Independence left financial chaos in its wake: the 13 states suffered Weimar-levels of inflation because they had printed unsecured paper with reckless abandon. And it took all of Alexander Hamilton's financial genius, his knowledge of

British best practice, and British investment to bring order out of chaos and lay the foundations for modern American capitalism. As Treasury Secretary, Hamilton created the first Bank of the United States, modeled closely on the Bank of England. To achieve the financial stability necessary to attract the British investment that was in turn essential to help pay off the American debt, Hamilton once again turned to the British model of monetizing the national debt by issuing long-term bonds that could be traded on the open market. And as Hamilton studied the British financial system in 1789, he also borrowed William Pitt's idea of the sinking fund — earmarking a portion of annual tax revenues to pay off the national debt. This helped tame rampant inflation resulting from the War of Independence and restored investor confidence. Building on the investor confidence established by Hamilton, British capital financed the construction of the American railroads — which knitted a continent into a country — and also financed much else of the American Industrial Revolution.

Pillar III: Diplomatic and Security Partnership.

The third and final pillar is the unique diplomatic and security partnership formed by the two countries. Since World War II, there has been a unique collaboration in defense and national security between Britain and the United States and in the closeness of our consultation and action about most world crises.

FDR and Churchill invented this unique defense and intelligence relationship, of course. They not only gave it its unique flavor, but also helped create the vast network of institutions and consultative arrangements to sustain the partnership. It would be absurd to suggest that a special relationship of this kind existed before 1941. But the theme of confronting the common adversary was not new to Anglo-American relations. It had existed since the 18th century as a shared assumption of common interest even when bilateral relations between Washington and London were strained. There are two striking examples of this. The first can be found in the foreign policy of the Federalists in the 1780s and the 1790s; the second even more striking example can be found in the foreign policy of Theodore Roosevelt and Lord Salisbury when there was a Falklands in reverse.

As John Lamberton Harper has argued, in the late 1780s and 1790s, John Jay, Alexander Hamilton, and George Washington created and implemented a prudent, realistic foreign policy of strength through peace. It was a foreign policy anchored in the belief that America's best interests lay in an alliance with Britain based on common interests. Like their counterparts in the British government, Hamilton, Jay, and Washington saw it as an irreducible interest of the United States, as well as Britain, to prevent the domination of the European continent by any single power. They saw British financial and naval power as America's first line of defense against French and Spanish ambitions to control the Mississippi Valley, thereby threatening the territorial integrity of the United States.

This policy found expression in Jay's Treaty in 1794, which represented the culmination of their earlier efforts to foster reconciliation based on reciprocity and shared interests and a common desire to heal the wounds of the Revolutionary War. Jay's Treaty not only repudiated the Franco-American alliance of 1778, but also marked the birth of a common Anglo-American strategic outlook and the hesitant beginnings of a mutual understanding. It also linked American and British security policy because it recognized that the Royal Navy was America's first line of defense against potential aggressors like France and Spain.

This said, it must be admitted that the 19th century was a difficult period for Anglo-American relations. Despite the best efforts of John Jay and Alexander Hamilton to heal the wounds of the Revolutionary War, this tragic conflict left a bitter legacy of mistrust. The War of 1812, another unnecessary war, made it worse. But in the decades before the Civil War, Anglo-American relations improved because Britain and the United States supported Latin American independence and opposed French and Spanish attempts to reconquer their former colonies.

The main source of friction arose out of the American Civil War and Britain's ambivalent response to it. While some British leaders, including then Prime Minister Lord Palmerston, hoped that the Civil War might lead to the breakup of the Union, the overwhelming majority wanted to keep out of the war. The ambivalence of British policy had deeper roots, however. On the one hand, the British anti-slavery movement (which had helped finance the American "underground-railroad" enabling slaves to escape to the North) had convinced almost all Britons that slavery must be abolished, and it lobbied successfully against recognition of the Confederacy. On the other, the powerful British textile industry needed continued access to cheap raw cotton, and the bankers of the City of London had to protect their loans to the big cotton plantation owners. Add to that the pressure from the large British shipbuilders eager to accommodate Confederate orders for warships, and one gets an idea of how difficult it was for the British government to formulate a consistent and balanced policy that did not offend either side in the Civil War.

But the British policy of nonrecognition was compromised by its decision to allow the Confederates to order warships from British shipyards. One such ship, the *Alabama*, built in the Cammell Laird shipyard on Merseyside, reached Confederate hands and sank nearly 60 Union vessels in 2 years. Afterwards, the victorious North was understandably angry that the British government had allowed the building of the *Alabama* and two other warships. What was important was not the dispute, but how it was resolved through a Joint High Commission. The Commission, whose actions personified the shared pragmatic Anglo-American common law tradition, agreed on suitable compensation for the damage caused by the *Alabama* and resolved the other outstanding grievances. Once again, the common law heritage helped ensure a joint approach and a successful resolution of a difficult, divisive problem.

Throughout the later part of the 19th century, despite the frictions caused by embittered Irish-Americans, Anglo-American relations grew much closer. There were three reasons for this. First, the passage of time and deft British diplomacy combined to soften Britain's image as the colonial oppressor and enemy of American independence. Second, America's remarkable economic growth after the Civil War created new opportunities for British investors, which they eagerly snapped up, thereby strengthening the Anglo-American business relationship. Third, the arrival of steam-powered transatlantic liners, combined with changes in British and American social structure, facilitated closer social relationships between the elites of both countries. America's new Gilded Age millionaires wanted the social prestige of links to the British aristocracy, which needed an infusion of American dollars to meet the ever-increasing costs of maintaining their vast country mansions. Between 1895 and 1903, the daughters of more than 70 American millionaires married prominent British aristocrats, many of them in key positions in government. The great Anglo-American rapprochement did indeed build on the these closer links, but it was driven primarily by a common strategic outlook: both governments agreed on the "Open Door" policy in China, and were deeply concerned about the emergence of an aggressive militaristic Germany in Europe and in the Pacific. Both governments saw each other as key allies in containing German power. U.S. Ambassador and later Secretary of State John Hay spoke for both governments when he wrote, "There is in the German mind something monstrous in the thought that a war should take place anywhere and they not profit by it." Lord Salisbury saw the Spanish-American War in 1898 as an excellent opportunity for a show of solidarity with the United States. Just after the outbreak of hostilities, Lord Salisbury's government not only declared its political support for the United States, but also gave the U.S. Navy the use of British bases in the Caribbean. The Royal Navy also gave Admiral Dewey every possible assistance in Hong Kong as he prepared to attack the Spanish fleet in the Philippines. It was truly a Falklands in reverse. So as the 20th century began and America stepped forcefully onto the world stage for the first time, she did so with Britain's full diplomatic, intelligence, and military support. The impact on U.S. leaders was profound. President Theodore Roosevelt (TR) wrote to his closest British friend, Cecil Spring Rice, "I am greatly mistaken if we ever slide back into the old conditions of bickering and angry mistrust." TR was right. We never have.

CONCLUSION

I hope I have provided a clue to unraveling the mystery of the special relationship. Before 1941, there was, of course, bickering and hostility, but underlying geopolitics and a common heritage continue to be inescapable. Both countries were always wary of expansionism on or from the European continent, so the implied partnership was always there. But it took the Nazi threat and the leadership of FDR and Churchill to make it explicit. They succeeded in building so well and so fast because the foundations were already there, strong and deeply rooted. Then and now, we are indeed "bound by a tie we did not forge and which we cannot break." Or, as Margaret Thatcher put it in an address to the Joint Houses of Congress on February 20, 1985,

> Our two countries have a common heritage as well as a common language. It is no mere figure of speech to say that many of your most enduring traditions — representative government, Habeas Corpus, trial by jury, a system of constitutional checks and balances — stem from our own small islands. But they are as much your lawful inheritance as ours. You did not borrow these traditions: you took them with you, because they were already your own.

SECTION I:

ECONOMIC AND BUSINESS ASPECTS
OF THE SPECIAL RELATIONSHIP

CHAPTER 2

THE SPECIAL RELATIONSHIP — ECONOMIC AND BUSINESS ASPECTS: AMERICAN PERSPECTIVE

Michael Calingaert

What constitutes a "special relationship"? And, particularly, what is "special"? Is it "distinctive"? "Unusual" or "unique"? Does it make a value judgment, connoting a relationship that is more important than other bilateral relationships? If so, how does one define or measure the scale of importance? Is it a relationship between governments, between peoples, or both? Is it a relationship that is distinguished by being privileged or preferential in some sense? If so, how? Or is the United States' relationship with every country "special" — perhaps some simply more "special" than others?

These are questions that underlie the assessment one is asked to make about the nature of a U.S.-UK relationship characterized as being "special." Viewed from the economic/business perspective, the relationship is, in many respects, distinctive and, in some respects, unique. On the other hand, many aspects of the relationship fit the pattern of U.S. relations with other countries of the developed world.

A related issue is American and British attitudes toward the existence of such a special relationship. To what extent does promoting the existence of and drawing attention to this special relationship promote national interests? What advantages are gained from doing so? While any such relationship is necessarily complex, and thus generalization can be misleading, the United Kingdom, as the smaller of the two partners, must compete for U.S. attention to enhance its influence over U.S. economic policies, particularly foreign economic policy, and promote its trade and investment objectives. Thus, there are clear advantages to the United Kingdom in propagating the idea that a special relationship exists, which is presumably why special relationship rhetoric is more prevalent there than in the United States. Of course, it is also important for the United States to obtain support for its foreign economic policies and to achieve its trade and investment goals. However, the United Kingdom plays a less important role relatively for the United States than the other way around. In any event, there is a downside for the United States in touting a special relationship—for it implies that other bilateral relationships are less "special."

CONTEXT OF THE RELATIONSHIP

Two essential constituents distinguish economic interaction between the United States and United Kingdom. In one respect, the economic relationship is distinctive and important to both sides, while in the other, it is less so.

The key of the U.S.-UK economic special relationship is the shared belief in and practice of what is often called the "Anglo-Saxon economic model" (while one can debate the appropriateness of this term, the intended distinction is between it and the more regulated form of capitalism prevailing in much of continental Europe). It refers to a web of laws, practices, and attitudes that reflect acceptance of a business culture and system that facilitate entrepreneurial activity (and permits failure), encourages wealth accumulation, promotes competition, and provides flexibility in the use of labor and other inputs.

The "model" contains many elements. One is a relatively reduced role of government as a participant in and, especially, regulator of the economy. Another is the preponderant role played by the stock and bond markets as a source for investment capital—compared to the Continent, where the banking system is more heavily involved—and, related to that, the high percentage of shareholding by the general public, which thus has a direct stake in the economy. A third is the similarities of the two countries' legal and accounting systems. Fourth is the strength of the financial services sector, consisting of a vast array of market participants ranging from financial intermediaries and accountants to insurance and pension funds. And, finally, the economies operate in a relatively transparent manner. This is perhaps more so in the United States than the United Kingdom in regard to the government and, increasingly, the private sector, as corporate governance issues assume ever greater prominence.

For the United States, these elements represent an essentially continuous pattern of policy and practice, whereas in the United Kingdom, they are the result of a significant measure of policies promoted by and adopted under the prime ministership of Margaret Thatcher in the 1980s, and, after their success became apparent, continued by the Labour government under Tony Blair. The net result of the mutual embrace of this economic model is a strong tendency to look at economic issues — domestic and international — from a similar point of view.

However — and this is the second constituent — this similarity of system and outlook is to some extent counterbalanced by UK membership in the European Union (EU). The United Kingdom is thus not a free agent in terms of economic policies and actions. EU economic integration has progressed to a remarkable degree. The EU single market, while clearly deficient in many areas, is nonetheless a reality over a wide range of economic activities. The EU has competence in major areas, notably competition policy and trade policy. Thus, the United Kingdom is but one of 25 member states making an input to those policies. Similarly, the voluminous corpus of EU law and regulation, the *acquis communautaire*, covers economic subjects, and the United Kingdom, like all member states, is bound by them. Thus, the freedom of action of the United Kingdom is, in many respects, limited.

Nonetheless, there is an important exception; that is the British "opt-out," i.e., nonparticipation, in the EU's Economic and Monetary Union, whose central feature is the single currency. This sets the United Kingdom apart — and enables it to play an independent role — in a major area of economic activity, one where the U.S.-UK bilateral relationship is unique, as will be described below. With that exception, however, the economic counterpart of the United States is, in large measure, the EU rather than the United Kingdom, or, indeed, any of the other EU member states. Thus, the United States cannot interact in the economic area with the United Kingdom in isolation from the EU, which means dealing with the European Commission and many or all of the member states.

PRIVATE SECTOR RELATIONSHIP

Trade.

The simplest measure of bilateral economic interaction is trade—a significant, though not special, relationship. The United Kingdom consistently has been an important trading partner of the United States. In terms of trade in goods, the United Kingdom is currently the fourth ranking overseas U.S. partner—not counting its contiguous neighbors, Canada and Mexico—after Japan, China, and Germany. It accounts for 3.6 percent of total U.S. goods trade, about the same level as Korea, amounting to just over $80 billion per year.[1] However, the composition of U.S.-UK trade has changed dramatically from goods to services, a trend that is likely to continue. In this sector, the United Kingdom, which accounts for 12 percent of world trade in services, ranks as the biggest U.S. trading partner.[2]

Regarding total trade flows in the two directions, the United Kingdom was the destination for 4.3 percent of U.S. exports in 2004, while imports from the United Kingdom were a smaller share of the total—3.1 percent. Interestingly, these shares are lower than those achieved in recent years: export share peaked at 5.3-5.7 percent in 1997-2001, while imports fell within the 3.4-3.8 percent range during the period 1991-2002.[3]

Investment.

Trade is, however, a much narrower indicator of economic interaction than investment. Intracompany trade accounts for a significant share of total trade, and sales by foreign affiliates dwarf trade volumes. In addition, of course, investment relations are deeper and more lasting than trade.

Looked at in terms of both investment flows and stock of investment, the United Kingdom is the top destination for U.S. direct investment. In 2004, over $23 billion was invested in the United Kingdom, amounting to 10 percent of U.S. worldwide investment and 28 percent of its investment in Western Europe. The total stock of U.S. investment in the United Kingdom is almost $300 billion, a figure approximately 30 percent greater than that in the next most important destination, Canada.[4] Over one million people in the United Kingdom work for U.S.-owned companies. Small and medium-sized U.S. enterprises participate very actively in this investment.[5]

By the same token, the United Kingdom predominates as a destination for U.S. investment in the EU. Except for one "bad" year (2001), the United Kingdom accounted for between 28 percent and 49 percent of annual U.S. foreign direct investment (FDI) that flowed into the EU during the 10-year period from 1994 to 2003. Similarly, when measuring the stock of U.S. FDI in the same period (without excluding 2001), the United Kingdom has accounted for a range of 32-41 percent in the EU. Of possible significance, both shares (the United Kingdom as a destination of U.S. FDI in the EU and in the world) peaked in the late 1990s; nevertheless, the United Kingdom easily maintained its number one position. [6]

The attractions of the United Kingdom as a destination for U.S. investment are many—some tangible, others less so. A common language and, to a somewhat lesser extent, common culture rank high on the list. The business environment is clearly favorable: the United Kingdom offers a well-developed infrastructure, receptivity to inward investment (and more generally to "outsiders" doing business in the United Kingdom), a political and legal system that offers confidence to investors that they will be equitably treated, ease of entry (and departure), low taxes, a skilled and well-educated workforce, labor flexibility, a strong research and development (R&D) sector, and, finally, an intangible but significant factor of comfort level. [7]

In the early stages of the EU, the United Kingdom was viewed by many U.S. companies as a gateway or staging area into what began as a customs union and then developed into an increasingly integrated economic area. However, over time the attraction of the United Kingdom was reduced by rising costs, competition from other destinations (notably Ireland, which featured low taxes, a common language, and a plentiful and well-educated workforce), and American firms' increasing comfort with locating elsewhere in the EU. Thus, there has been some increase in investment in the rest of the EU. Reflecting the decline in manufacturing in the United

Kingdom, the share of that sector in U.S. investment in the United Kingdom has fallen from 39 percent to 15 percent. However, the decline was offset by other attractive areas, with most of that money moving into the finance, information technology, and property sectors.[8]

One factor potentially affecting investment in the United Kingdom is the British opt-out of the single currency, and its continued reluctance to join. The "drying up" of inward investment predicted by some when the Euro was introduced, without UK participation, has not taken place. However, the further away British entry into the Economic and Monetary Union seems, the more likely investment in the United Kingdom—not only by U.S. firms—will be adversely affected. That will be particularly so if the UK economy ceases to outperform that of the Eurozone. Observers in the United Kingdom report that Britain's opt-out has not been a major factor in inward investment decisions thus far, as most investors have assumed that the United Kingdom will eventually join the eurozone. However, firms that operate on small margins and are currency sensitive are concerned about the situation.

Another potentially negative factor in U.S. investment decisions is the further development of EU social legislation—regulating many of the conditions of employment and the rights of workers—and its extension to the United Kingdom. Although the United Kingdom received an opt-out from this legislation, there are pressures within the EU to terminate this exemption. Were the exemption to be rescinded, the attractiveness of the United Kingdom as a destination for U.S. investment would be diminished. Still, developments in these two areas—the future of the single currency and social legislation— may be affected by the crisis within the EU as a result of the French and Dutch rejection of the draft EU Constitution.

On the other side of the ledger, the United Kingdom remains a popular site for U.S. companies. An estimated 7,500 U.S. firms have offices in the United Kingdom. Of these, 500 are corporate headquarters, often of regional operations. It is estimated that one-half of U.S. companies with corporate offices in Europe have located those offices in the United Kingdom.[9]

Tourism.

The United Kingdom is the most important U.S. partner in two-way tourism. Although U.S. residents travel more frequently to Canada and Mexico, expenditures on travel and transportation are highest for visits to the United Kingdom. In 2000, more than four million Americans spent over $11 billion traveling to the United Kingdom, compared with $7.5 billion (the second highest sum) in Mexico. In the other direction, British visitors to the United States number annually just under five million and spend almost $13 billion, figures that place it only slightly below Japan.[10]

Financial Market.

Here is perhaps where the "special economic relationship" is most evident — indeed, the word "unique" is not out of place. The historical ties between American and British capital date back to the 19th century, when British investment played an important role in the economic development of the United States. Banking relationships have a long history; many banks were well-established in the other's country in the period between the two world wars, if not before.

One can speak of a single financial market, located in London and New York. Each is a financial powerhouse, and each is an undisputed financial center — London in Europe and New York in the United States. The New York Stock Exchange is the biggest stock exchange in the world, and it, together with New York-based Nasdaq, gives the United States its preeminent position for stock trading. London manages almost half of Europe's institutional equity capital, and 70 percent of Eurobonds are traded in London. It is also the world's largest international insurance and foreign exchange market.[11]

American and British financial institutions are major players in the world, accustomed to working globally. The U.S. investment banking community has acquired a preeminent position in London, while UK commercial banks are very competitive and present globally. Of the world's top 15 "tier one capital" banks, over one-half are American or British (four banks each).[12] There are more American banks in London than in New York (a reflection of the prevalence of U.S. regional — not New York — banks that have international operations).

These developments were facilitated by the similarity of economic and legal systems and the role of stock and bond markets in the two countries. It also has spurred the expansion of American-British ties in other related sectors, notably insurance and law firms.

In one manifestation of this relationship, U.S. bank claims on and liabilities to the United Kingdom are vast, second only to the Cayman Islands. U.S. claims on the United Kingdom and Cayman Islands at the end of 2004 were both about half a trillion dollars, with the next country, the Bahamas, accounting for only about one-fifth of that amount. U.S. liabilities to the British were about $430 billion (for the Cayman Islands, it was double that figure). The total U.S. banking relationship (claims and liabilities) with the United Kingdom has grown from the equivalent of 10 percent of world trade in 1978 to 19 percent in 2004.[13]

Defense Industry.

Although close relationships exist in a number of industrial sectors, probably none is closer than in the defense industry. However, unlike the other sectors, government policies and actions largely determine the nature and extent of the relationship. Closely held and subject to government control, U.S. defense technology sharing takes place at a higher level with the United Kingdom than with virtually any other country (Australia and Canada also vie for that position).

Trade in defense equipment is significant, and it flows in both directions. American firms are routinely invited to bid on British defense tenders, and they have registered many successes. The United Kingdom is by far the largest overseas buyer of American products. Major British purchases have included the Apache helicopter, Airborne Warning and Control System (AWACS), and Airborne Stand-off Radar (ASTOR). Moreover, the United Kingdom is the launch customer for the C-130J aircraft.

By the same token, UK companies are among the most active participants in the "special security arrangement," under which U.S.-based subsidiaries of foreign companies can be certified to bid as subcontractors on U.S. tenders. The most notable recent instance was the U.S. Navy's decision in early 2005 to accept the Lockheed-

Martin-led bid for the new Presidential helicopter fleet, which includes a British component.

Significant shares of the U.S. market are held by such British firms as Rolls Royce, Martin Baker, and Smith Industries. However, the leading British player is BAE, the fifth largest supplier of hardware to the U.S. military (and the largest foreign supplier). Like other British firms, BAE has been looking to increase its business opportunities in the United States. Its recent multibillion dollar purchases include Lockheed-Martin's electronic assets and United Defense Industries, the latter ($3.5 billion) being the largest foreign takeover of an American defense company. By any measure, BAE is a significant player in the U.S. defense industry sector, employing over 25,000 in its U.S. operations.

A further example of close cooperation is the Joint Strike Fighter project, in which the United Kingdom is a major partner. BAE is an associate prime contractor, participating in the work and technology on the new aircraft, which will be purchased by both governments.

The dispute that erupted in 2004 between the United States and the EU over the possible lifting of the latter's embargo on arms sales to China placed the British defense industry in a delicate position. While it did not want to forgo business opportunities in China, at the same time it did not want to jeopardize existing and potential business and the transfer of technology with the United States. On balance, the latter consideration prevailed, and BAE, for one, announced publicly it would not participate in trade with China. The British government generally reflected industry's position, at first going along with the French and German-led initiative to lift the embargo, but backing away quickly when vociferous U.S. opposition surfaced.

GOVERNMENT-TO-GOVERNMENT RELATIONSHIP

Multilateral.

The world's multilateral economic agenda is vast, and so is the range of multilateral institutions that deal with it. Both the U.S. and UK governments interact on these many issues as they operate in a multilateral context.

In general, the two governments convey similar messages on issues relating to the world economy—what policies national governments should follow to enhance economic growth, operation of the international monetary system, trade policy, operation of the international financial institutions, and the like—in the course of what might be called normal international discourse, including more specifically the G-7/G-8 and the Organization for Economic Cooperation and Development (OECD). On the whole, the United States and United Kingdom work together in those forums to promote their mutual interests.

In some areas, however, there is a significant difference in policy. The most notable example is the environment, particularly in attitudes toward the Kyoto Convention. The United Kingdom has agreed with the consensus view within the EU—and indeed virtually the rest of the world—and worked toward the adoption of the Convention, while the United States has firmly refused to accede to it. Nonetheless, the United Kingdom accepts that the United States will not accede to Kyoto, and thus seeks to find common ground in other aspects of environmental policy.

On the other hand, the two governments have traditionally seen eye-to-eye on trade, where they have been leaders in efforts to build and maintain a liberal trading system, including the current work on the Doha multilateral trading round. However, on trade, the United Kingdom cannot carry out an independent policy because competence for trade lies with the EU. Thus, the United Kingdom remains one voice out of 25—albeit a strong and influential one—on all trade issues. Nonetheless, that has not prevented U.S. and UK negotiators on the Doha round from working closely together.

European Union.

The United States and EU have grappled with a host of trade disputes over the years, while at the same time enjoying an unprecedented and flourishing economic relationship (a sometimes-overlooked, but critical, fact). Looking through the list of recent issues, one finds some concordance of position, but also many instances where the United States and the United Kingdom are on opposite sides of the argument.

- *EU regulation of chemical substances*: With similar industrial interests and views on regulation (less is better than more), the two governments have fought for an extensive watering-down of the proposal of the European Commission for registering, evaluating, and authorizing chemicals (REACH).

- *U.S. foreign sales corporation*: In the long struggle over U.S. legislation, the United Kingdom played a constructive role in the ultimately successful effort to keep the issue from getting out of control, giving the United States leeway in terms of time and modalities for settlement. Following the adoption of new tax provisions in the United States, the British government sought to prevent a return of the issue to the World Trade Organization (WTO) and the reimposition of sanctions by the EU.

- *EU banana regime*: The United Kingdom historically protected the banana exports of its former colonies in the Caribbean at the expense of Latin American producers, and thus it was not particularly sympathetic to U.S. efforts to prevent a restrictive EU regime from replacing the various national regimes. However, it believed the EU should comply with the WTO ruling in favor of the United States, a view that was reinforced by U.S. retaliation against imported cashmere sweaters.

- *Biotechnology/genetically-modified organisms*: In the long-running U.S.-EU battles over a number of issues in this area, the United Kingdom generally has supported the U.S. view that decisions should be based on scientific evidence, despite strong opposition from the British public that is very "pro-environmentalist."

- *U.S. safeguard action against steel imports*: Like the rest of the EU, the United Kingdom, which exports significant quantities of specialty steel to the United States, sharply criticized President Bush's first-term action (subsequently rescinded). It pressed for, and received, exemptions from the increased tariffs.

- *Airbus subsidies*: As a major participant in the Airbus consortium, the United Kingdom has stoutly defended Airbus against U.S. allegations of unfair subsidization and

27

criticized what it considers to be comparable subsidies by the U.S. military to U.S. commercial aircraft manufacturers. Nonetheless, it favors a negotiated settlement rather than seeking recourse to the WTO.

- *EU's Common Agricultural Policy* (CAP): Because of the nature of its agriculture and its domestic agricultural policy, the United Kingdom has been among the sharpest internal critics of the CAP, thus lending support to the United States in its long-standing efforts to reduce the distortions it has caused to world agricultural trade. Prime Minister Blair made this clear in the EU budgetary dispute in June 2005.

- *Regulatory convergence*: This is a major undertaking designed to reduce the impediments arising from differences in regulatory regimes in the United States and EU. While American and British regulators generally share a similar regulatory philosophy, some problems have arisen from differences between the regulatory structures in the two countries. The United Kingdom has been bothered by the reluctance of the U.S. Securities and Exchange Commission to recognize decisions of British regulators and the problems caused by regulation of insurance at the state, rather than national, level. On the other side, U.S. regulators occasionally have felt that the UK Financial Services Authority has not adopted sufficiently tough positions in the EU, where it plays an influential role.

Whether in agreement or not, there is intense, extensive, and positive interaction between the two governments. U.S. government officials have found their British counterparts to be open and helpful. The British are good sources of information on the inner workings of the EU for their American colleagues. However, this occurs primarily when the two governments are on the same side of an issue. Not surprisingly, when they are not, the United Kingdom is considerably less helpful.

Traditionally, there has been a tendency for some parts of the U.S. government to assume that the United Kingdom is on its side on issues under consideration at the EU, and that the British can, or should, be counted on to promote U.S. views. As seen above, the first premise is by no means universally correct. While overall the British outlook and objectives are in accord with those of the United States, on many specific issues that simply is not the case. With regard to the British role inside the EU, the United Kingdom is an active and influential player in the EU deliberations. Suspect in the eyes of many other members for Britain's "outsider" status—i.e., opt-out of the Euro and generally weak support for further integration and market regulation—British officials have to take care not to be perceived by other member states as carrying water for the United States as they pursue UK policy objectives.

Bilateral.

Significant bilateral economic differences are rare. The major exception is the civil aviation relationship. This relationship is governed by a long-standing bilateral agreement, Bermuda II, which specifies the conditions under which American and British carriers can operate between the two countries. It has long been a bone of contention, with the United States chafing under what it considers to be unduly restrictive provisions, particularly as regards access of its carriers to Heathrow Airport; and the United Kingdom complaining about U.S. restrictions on foreign ownership of U.S. airlines and the ban on foreign carriers flying between points inside the United States. The United Kingdom has stoutly resisted U.S. efforts to bring the bilateral agreement more closely into accord with the series of "open skies" regimes it has negotiated with almost all European countries in recent years. However, after an unsuccessful 2-plus year effort to renegotiate Bermuda II bilaterally, the issue will move from the bilateral to the EU sphere. The European Court of Justice has confirmed that civil aviation agreements fall within the competence of the EU, rather than the individual member states, and thus this issue will be added to the U.S.-EU portfolio.

CONCLUSIONS AND POLICY RECOMMENDATIONS

The U.S. economic and business relationship with the United Kingdom is without any doubt among its most important. The

United Kingdom is a major economic partner, both in the public and private spheres. In some respects the relationship is distinctive, unique, and — yes — special.

Are there ways this relationship can be improved, i.e., rendered more effective in meeting the two countries' objectives? On the business side, the answer is probably "not to any significant extent." The framework within which businesses operate and business decisions are made is firmly established, well-known, and not notably in need of change. On the government-to-government side, there is little apparent need for structural or institutional change. The governments know each other well and communicate freely and frequently.

The one area where improvement could be made is the quality of government-to-government interaction. This has two aspects. First, exchanges between American and British bureaucrats should be expanded. A program similar to the existing exchange of U.S. and British diplomats, under which Americans serve a tour in the Foreign and Commonwealth Office and British do likewise at the State Department, should be introduced for the UK Department of Trade and Industry and the Treasury. In addition, British bureaucrats visiting Washington should regularly add the U.S. Congress to their schedule. Both sides can profit from an improved understanding of the other's points of view and positions in the decisionmaking process .

Second, the selection of the American ambassador to the United Kingdom should be made on the basis of competence rather than political indebtedness, as has almost invariably been the case. Unless the function of the ambassador is deemed to be superfluous to bilateral dialogue and interaction — certainly not the view of the British government, which has invariably sent its most qualified diplomat — it behooves the United States to send ambassadors with the experience and skills to promote U.S. interests and enhance this special relationship, whether it be a career or a noncareer person. Indeed, at this time of heightened transatlantic misunderstanding, it is all the more essential for the United States to field an ambassador who can articulate U.S. policy and seek to influence government policy and public opinion abroad.

Finally, in the EU context, it is essential that the remarkably effective relationship between American and European trade negotiators Robert Zoellick and Pascal Lamy be replicated by their successors. The personalities of their successors, Peter Mandelson and Robert Portman, give grounds for hope, but only time will tell how effectively their relationship works as they grapple with a range of difficult issues, which will necessarily affect the bilateral relationship between the United States and the United Kingdom.

ENDNOTES - CHAPTER 2

1. U.S. Census Bureau, "Top Trading Partners – Total Trade, Exports, Imports," published February 2005, *http://www.census.gov/foreign-trade/statistics/highlights/top/top0412.html*.

2. U.S. Bureau of Economic Analysis, "U.S. International Services: Cross-Border Trade 1986-2003, and Sales Through Affiliates, 1986-2002," published October 2004, *http://www.bea.gov/bea/di/1001serv/intlserv.htm*.

3. *Ibid.*

4. On a historical cost basis. U.S. Bureau of Economic Analysis, "U.S. Direct Investment Abroad: Balance of Payments and Direct Investment Position Data," published March 2005, *http://www.bea.doc.gov/bea/di/di1usdbal.htm*.

5. British-American Business, Inc.

6. U.S. Bureau of Economic Analysis.

7. *Ibid.*

8. Union des Industries de la Communaute europeenne (UNICE).

9. American Embassy, London.

10. U.S. Bureau of Transportation Statistics, *U.S. International Travel and Transportation Trends*, 2002.

11. *London as a Financial Centre*, from *http://www.london.gov.uk/london-life/business-and-jobs/financial-centre.jsp*.

12. The Banker, 2004, *Top 1000 World Banks*, from *http://www.thebanker.com/news/fullstory.php/aid/1699/Top_1000_World_Banks.html*.

13. U.S. Department of the Treasury, Treasury International Capital System, "U.S. Banking Liabilities to Foreigners" and "U.S. Banking Claims on Foreigners," published April 2005, *http://www.treas.gov/tic/ticliab.html* and *http://www.treas.gov/tic/ticl*.

CHAPTER 3

ANGLO-AMERICAN ECONOMIC AND BUSINESS RELATIONSHIPS: A BRITISH PERSPECTIVE

Ray Raymond

The great British Prime Minister Lord Salisbury is said to have remarked to Her Majesty Queen Victoria, "Change, change, why do we need more change? Aren't things bad enough already?"

As one of the architects of the Anglo-American rapprochement at the end of the 19th century, Lord Salisbury would be delighted by the revitalization of the British economy and the strengthening of the Anglo-American economic relationship over the past 25 years, and especially over the last 8. They completely refute the conclusions of the influential Wilson Center–Ditchley Foundation conferences published in 1988 that Britain's importance to the United States as an economic partner was diminishing rapidly. Simply put, the Wilson-Ditchley analysis — understandable in the context of the times — was that the United Kingdom (UK) was sinking into increasing poverty because of its declining productivity and competitiveness. In broader strategic terms, therefore, Britain was counting for less and less, and its ability to function as an effective strategic partner for the United States was almost at an end.

What a difference the consistent and rigorous application of sound fiscal, micro, and macro economic and monetary policies make. Today, in 2005, Britain is experiencing the longest period of continuous economic growth and increased living standards seen in the past half a century. As UK Chancellor Gordon Brown said in his budget speech earlier this year, "Britain begins the 21st century from a firm foundation of the lowest inflation for 30 years, the lowest interest rates for 40 years, and the highest level of employment in our history. Unlike the United States, the Eurozone, and Japan, the British economy has grown uninterrupted every quarter over the past 6 years."

Despite the world economic downturn of 2001-02, Britain has overtaken France as the world's fourth largest economy and, if current economic trends continue, some experts believe the UK could overtake Germany as the world's third largest economy by about 2012. Perhaps the most telling statistics are that British unemployment is approximately half that in the Eurozone; that unlike the United States, the UK actually gained jobs during the slowdown of 2001-02; that the UK's productivity per capita has overtaken Japan and is poised to overtake Germany. Britain still lags far behind the United States in productivity, but continues to learn from American innovation, competition, and enterprise.

There are two main reasons for this dramatic transformation: the first is the supply-side reforms of the Thatcher years, supplemented by those of Gordon Brown since 1997; the second is the new monetary and fiscal framework introduced in 1997 which has helped create a stronger, more flexible, more enterprising Britain. UK monetary and fiscal policy has responded successfully to the recent world economic downturn and kept the British economy stable and growing. This economically resurgent Britain is a more important economic partner for the United States than at any time since the beginning of the 20th century.

The Private Sector Relationship.

The first key feature of the U.S.-UK economic special relationship is the remarkable interpenetration of the two economies. Today, more than half of the total earnings of U.S. overseas investors are accounted for by Europe. And, within Europe, the UK is overwhelmingly the most important single national market for corporate America. On average, about 40 percent of all U.S. investment in Europe goes to the UK. British officials estimate that over 60 percent of American companies doing business in the European Union (EU) have their European headquarters in the UK. During the 1990s, U.S. investment in the United Kingdom (at $175 billion) was nearly 50 percent larger than the total invested by American firms in the whole Asia-Pacific region.

Of course, U.S. firms are investing very large sums in China, India, and Brazil, but what is little noticed is that America's stock of assets in the UK alone is almost equal to the combined overseas affiliate base of U.S. firms in Asia, Latin America, Africa, and the

Middle East. In an average year, total sales by U.S. firms in the UK alone, at over $400 billion, are greater than aggregate U.S. sales in the whole of Latin America and almost double those in Germany.

And what about jobs? Today, U.S. firms employ about 1.3 million workers in Britain. That is more than the entire U.S. affiliate work force in all developing Asia and five times greater than those working for American firms in China. Moreover, the British return the compliment. Over 1.2 million Americans go to work each day in British-owned companies in the United States. And just as the United States is Britain's largest investor, so the UK by far is America's largest foreign investor, with total foreign direct investment (FDI) of over $280 billion.

If the investment relationship is special, the links between the London and New York financial markets are truly unique. The historical relationship between British and American capital dates back to the 18th century when British investment played an important role in the economic development of the original 13 colonies and in stabilizing U.S. public finances after the Revolutionary War. Later, British investment bankers provided much of the capital that financed America's phenomenal economic growth in the 19th century.

As Michael Calingaert writes in his contribution to this book, it is now possible to "speak of a single financial market located in London and New York. Each is a financial powerhouse," and all the evidence is that they will continue to dominate global financial markets for the rest of 21st century. Together, London and New York account for just over 50 percent of global foreign exchange dealing, 92 percent of foreign equity trading, and 28 percent of cross-border bank lending. London is the world leader in fund management, New York a close second. New York is the global leader in mergers and acquisitions, London second. Their shared dominance is underpinned by the shared Anglo-American legal systems that govern such a large portion of international mergers and acquisitions and public stock offerings. Their shared dominance is reinforced by the UK-U.S.-led surge in international mergers and acquisitions throughout the 1990s and by the UK-led move to privatization of publicly-owned services and utilities.

Above all, the London-New York link has been reinforced by globalization and, ironically, the introduction of the Euro.

Globalization has done three things to reinforce the unique New York-London partnership. The first is that it has encouraged the major players — Goldman Sachs, Citigroup, Merrill Lynch, HSBC — to have operations in both cities. The second is that globalization has compelled the big American investment houses to increase their operations in London because it is the best way to win more business in global markets. The third way globalization has reinforced the New York-London dominance is that it gives investors and issuers of stock what they both want: access to the widest range of global securities and investment products and a worldwide pool of global investors. The introduction of the Euro has also strengthened the New York-London link because it has encouraged more U.S. investment houses to see London as their base for European mergers and acquisitions work and to increase their presence there accordingly.

The Anglo-American Model.

The second special feature of Anglo-American economic relations is the remarkable breadth of agreement between contemporary U.S. administrations (Democrat or Republican) and contemporary British governments (Conservative or New Labour) over so many fundamental areas of economic policy. This level of agreement is the product of more than 20 years of convergence in thinking about economic policy and in results achieved. Britain has shaped U.S. thinking on deregulation, privatization of public services, and enterprise zones. The United States taught Britain the importance of flexible labor markets, welfare reform, and having an independent central bank responsible for monetary policy. Overall, the Anglo-American "model" aims to reduce the role of government as a regulator of economic activity and to change it from a provider to an enabler of services; to create flexible labor markets and entrepreneurship, promote competition, and encourage wealth accumulation through ownership of property and stocks, thereby creating an "ownership society." There are areas where we differ — the financing of health care being the most obvious. But what unites us is far more powerful than what divides us. In my judgment, what the Anglo-American model boils down to is: (1) the abandonment of the old-style socialist or Great Society welfare state in favor of free market capitalism, and (2) the belief that government should be an enabling force empowering, encouraging, and equipping its citizens to meet the challenges of globalization. Lest there be any doubt, compare the essence of President George W. Bush's compassionate conservatism with that of Prime Minister Tony Blair's Third Way. Here is Myron Magnet, the intellectual architect of compassionate conservatism on the welfare state: President Bush's campaign for Social Security reform "is part of the large and coherent worldview that has evolved out of compassionate conservatism. What has made America exceptional is limitless opportunity for everyone, at all levels — the chance to find a job, to advance up the ladder as you prove yourself, and to prosper. A giant welfare state hampers the job creation that makes all this opportunity possible. Bush is determined to keep the dynamism vibrant and to encourage and empower the poor to take part in it, rather than suggest that they are unequal to the task." And here is Tony Blair on the same topic: "The challenge of modern employment is about extending welfare to work, making work pay, and investing in the skills individuals need. In a more insecure and demanding labor market, it recognises that people will change jobs more often, and believes government has a vital role in equipping individuals to prosper." Unless I am badly mistaken, the President and the Prime Minister would agree with the recent comments of the White House Director of Strategic Initiatives: "Government's default position should not be to view citizens as wards of the state, but rather as responsible and independent, self-sufficient and upright."

And it is no accident that the two major economies which have performed best over the last decade are the two that have put this philosophy into practice: Britain and the United States. And because Britain and the United States have created this model, the two governments generally approach most domestic and international economic policy issues from a shared perspective.

In his chapter, Michael Calingaert suggests that, apart from civil aviation, there are very few differences between the two governments. This is true, but understates the closeness and intensity of the policy collaboration between London and Washington today in all the key multilateral forums, including the EU. The UK and United States not only share a common business model, but also a belief that they must lead the process of labor, capital, and product reform in Europe so that they can create a more open market across the Atlantic which will benefit the EU as well as the United States. The total annual two-way flow of foreign direct investment of goods and services between the United States and the EU is over $2.5 trillion, but it could be even higher.

The British and U.S. treasuries believe that if the United States and EU break down more of the remaining transatlantic barriers and create a more open market across the Atlantic, then this could bring about $350 billion in benefits for both the United States and the EU. How to get there? Faster removal of industrial tariffs and nontariff barriers, liberalization in services, labor market reforms, common accounting standards, and closer regulatory cooperation to prevent domestic regulators from putting up barriers to trade and causing needless conflicts.

Not surprisingly, elements of this reform agenda are key priorities for the British Presidency of the EU, including initiatives to reassess and, if necessary, roll back unnecessary regulation now damaging competitiveness; and strengthening systems used to monitor whether the benefits of proposed regulations outweigh the costs, etc. That Britain will be able to achieve any of these much needed reforms is highly questionable.

Britain, the United States, and the EU.

Unfortunately, the similarity of outlook, policy, and system between the United States and the United Kingdom is offset by British membership of the EU. This limits Britain's freedom of action especially in trade and competition policy, where, for better or worse, competence has been ceded to Brussels. As Michael Calingaert points out, the UK has had to absorb the entire corpus of EU law and regulation into its domestic law which, in my judgment, has often worked against the UK government's own efforts to embrace the challenges of globalization, forcing British Ministers and officials to spend enormous amounts of valuable time fighting the EU's damaging directives. The prolonged showdown over Britain's wise opt-out from the absurdly restrictive EU working time directive is just one example. Calingaert is right in pointing out that today in large measure, the U.S. economic counterpart is now the EU rather than the UK or, indeed, any of the 24 other EU member states. Whether that will continue to be the case remains to be seen. As the recent U.S. National Intelligence Council Report on the World in 2020 has correctly argued, continuing economic sclerosis in the Eurozone "could lead to the splintering or, at worst, the disintegration of the EU."

The crisis of confidence and direction which the EU now faces after the rejection of the EU Constitution by French and Dutch voters and the collapse of the its June 2005 Budget summit are about much more than economics. The crisis was brought on by profound anger over the EU's democratic deficit: the failure of European governments to consult their electorates about key decisions, combined with the lack of democratic accountability in the EU's own decisionmaking. It is a crisis brought about also by the failure of the European economic model to deliver jobs and prosperity, by enlargement, by the reemergence of nationalism, and by the rejection of the more integrationist vision of Europe's future. It is now clear that there exists a yawning chasm between the integrationist vision of European bureaucratic and political elites and the legitimate aspirations of their citizens to retain their national identity.

Above all, however, the truth is that globalization has thrown a harsh light on the failure of the Eurozone. Or, as Myron Magnet has rightly put it, "The failure of the European model . . . is one of the signal facts of our era. In Europe, the idea that capitalism creates a permanently jobless class has become a self-fulfilling prophecy, as strict regulation and the high taxes needed to pay lavish welfare and unemployment benefits have resulted in half the U.S. rate of job creation, twice the rate of unemployment, and much less opportunity." The Organization for Economic Cooperation and Development (OECD) agrees with Magnet, warning European leaders this summer that without labor market and welfare reform, the Eurozone is doomed to terminal economic decline.

The conclusion is clear: The Anglo-American model offers the only credible way forward, and its European critics should be honest enough to recognize that it is not the Dickensian bogeyman they like to say it is. For example, both Britain and the United States have increased national public spending on primary and secondary education and on health care. Both countries have also implemented welfare reform and reduced child poverty. As Blair argued in his masterful speech to the European Parliament on June 23, 2005, Europe can either huddle together under the bed covers hoping globalization will go away, or it can confront its challenges head on. But will it?

The evidence is not encouraging. Like the German voters of North Rhine Westphalia in May 2005, the voters of France and the Netherlands a month later emphatically rejected the structural reforms necessary to increase productivity and enhance competitiveness. *Financial Times* columnist Quentin Peel is surely right when he argues that "the prospects for embracing difficult economic reforms may be as moribund as those for ratifying the constitutional treaty."

Worse, the political influence of Britain, the one European power willing to fight for structural reform, has been seriously weakened by recent developments. In 2004, British influence appeared to be increasing. The defeat of the Franco-German-backed candidate for President of the European Commission, the election of the British-backed Barosso and his pro-growth, pro-reform agenda (much of which was shaped by British thinking), and the continuing economic failure of the Eurozone, suggested that the UK might be able to change the European agenda. This hope was reinforced because enlargement changed the correlation of forces within the EU by giving Britain new allies who wanted more open, flexible economies.

In April 2005, because of this background, I was far too optimistic in my presentation to the second of the two conferences on which this book is based. I thought that economic realism would prevail within the EU, but I was wrong. As I write in early July 2005, the EU is in utter disarray, and the prospects for real reform are more remote than ever. The regional election results in North Rhine Westphalia alluded to above showed that German voters deeply opposed even the initial steps towards labor market reform proposed by Chancellor Gerhard Schroeder. The referendum results in France and the Netherlands showed that the revolt against labor market reform was not confined to Germany. The EU crisis has been made worse by the failure of the recent Brussels summit, for which most Europeans blame Blair. The

Prime Minister's firm and justified insistence that any reduction in the British rebate must be linked to broader reform of the EU budget and the Common Agricultural Policy alienated even his closest allies in East-Central Europe. They were understandably upset because they needed a budget deal to release funds to help rebuild their economies. Most of them remain supportive of his reform agenda, but relations need to be repaired. Even when they are, however, the Prime Minister faces a much more difficult obstacle: weakened and defensive French and German governments. As Peel astutely put it: "Far from clearing the way for British leadership, such Franco-German weakness is more likely to guarantee gridlock." In other words, getting an EU-wide commitment to structural reform is further away than ever.

Conclusion.

In his speech to the European Parliament on June 24, 2005, Blair was right to warn that Europe faced "failure on a grand strategic scale" if it tried to hold back the forces of globalization and block the economic reforms necessary to save it from terminal economic decline. I believe that that moment of failure is already at hand: The core of the Eurozone is already many miles down the road to terminal decline, and neither its voters nor its elected leaders appear to have the political will to embrace the painful reforms necessary to reverse it. The result — as the U.S. National Intelligence Council predicts — will be the splintering and possible disintegration of the EU.

So where does that leave the special relationship? The short answer is that it becomes more special and more vital than ever. The interpenetration of our two dynamic economies is deeper than ever. The vast flows of investment between our two countries grow ever greater, and the London-New York dominance of world financial markets seems assured for the foreseeable future. Britain and the United States have never been more important economic partners for each other. Together they need to look beyond Europe to meet the challenge from the two sunrise economies of the 21st century: China and India. In addition to investing more in each other, this is where the United States and UK should be investing their financial and diplomatic resources.

CHAPTER 4

THE ECONOMIC AND BUSINESS DIMENSION: PANEL CHAIRMAN'S SUMMARY AND RECOMMENDATIONS

Erik R. Peterson

Look back 60 years, to the end of the Second World War, and imagine that it had marked too the end of the alliance between Europe and America. We would not have the great institutions which that alliance forged in the aftermath of war — the UN, NATO, the World Bank, the IMF. Without America's support, Europe's reconstruction would have been longer and more arduous; its democracies today far less firmly entrenched; and the unique enterprise of the European Union might never have got past the planning stage. The Cold War might not have been won — it might even have been lost, in Europe at least. The great wave of economic liberalization and political freedom which has so enriched billions of lives might have been no more than a ripple.

The words above were spoken on May 18, 2005, at my organization, the Center for Strategic and International Studies (CSIS), by UK Foreign Secretary Jack Straw, as part of a speech he entitled "A Partnership for Wider Freedom." Three months earlier, U.S. President George W. Bush had described the importance of U.S.-European relations this way: "Our strong friendship is essential to peace and prosperity across the globe — and no temporary debate, no passing disagreement of governments, no power on earth will ever divide us."[1]

Both these statements emphasize the significance of cooperation between Europe and the United States in a range of events that helped shape the world around us today, and by their nature and context imply that such cooperation is equally necessary if we are to confront effectively challenges that lie in the future. And by their respective contexts, they both clearly imply that the role of the United Kingdom (UK) in bridging Europe and America is as important today as it was 60 years ago.

This is the basis for the "special relationship" writ large, the relationship that bundles critical U.S. and UK political, security, economic, financial, and other interests across the Atlantic. It is also the basis for the relationship described by U.S. Undersecretary of State for Political Affairs Nicholas Burns soon after he assumed his most recent portfolio at the State Department: "As a career diplomat, I am convinced that our ability to succeed on this daunting agenda is directly related to our ability to work closely and productively with Europe. That is why it is fitting to start my tenure here in Europe — our indispensable partner — and specifically, in the United Kingdom, our most trusted and indispensable ally."[2]

In looking forward, the operative question is whether in a highly complex future environment, the United States and the UK can continue to give effect to these kinds of sweeping declaratory statements. The key uncertainty is whether the two countries will be able to maintain what has been "special" about their relations — whether the UK will be able to maintain its identity as both a member of the European Union (EU) and a close partner of the United States, and whether the United States will continue to regard the UK at once "part of" and yet "separate and distinct from" the rest of Europe. In the end, the challenge is to create the basis of a continued "special relationship" that will enable leaders to trumpet the benefits of cooperation, as Secretary Straw did last May, 60 years in the future. How well we succeed will depend on our capacity to "build a better and safer world through a renewed and reinvigorated alliance for freedom between Europe and the United States," as Secretary Straw observed in his speech at CSIS.

There can be little doubt that economic and commercial relations are at the core of the current "special relationship." The two countries have long been bound by significant and longstanding trade, investment, and business ties. And for good reason. First and most obvious, they speak the same language. But the depth of the relationship goes well beyond the common vocabulary of the English language. Owing to the shared grammar of the "Anglo-Saxon economic model" and commonly-held beliefs and practices when it comes to corporate culture, the level of effective interaction at both the government and private business levels has been pronounced. Then there is the "tense" of U.S.-UK relations — past, present, and future. The legacy of the special relationship itself is a foundation for the perpetuation of the "special ties" that exist. That both sides are building on a well-established pattern of cooperation shows that the relationship benefits from its own historical momentum.

As impressive as they are, the empirical data on trade, investment, and commercial cooperation only partially reflect the depth of the relationship. Overall U.S.-EU economic relations are unparalleled. In aggregate terms, the economic and commercial linkages between the United States and Europe total some $2.5 trillion. More importantly, the economies are inextricably linked at one level after the other—through cross-investment, employment, trade of goods and services, trade in services, capital flows, and so on. Furthermore, cooperation between the two largest economic entities on the planet[3] is a precondition for progress in dealing with the range of issues outside their direct relations, stretching from progress in trade liberalization through dealing with third-party states—in particular, the rapid emergence of China as a global economic force—to the Doha Development Round of the World Trade Organization and then to the various G-8 agendas. These agendas include, most recently, such important items as economic development in Africa and the spread of weapons of mass destruction.[4] Obviously, these dimensions of transatlantic relations are often overshadowed by more immediate political and security challenges, but the capacity of the two sides to work together on broader economic and economic development issues is essential to progress in a number of areas.[5]

Within this context of overall U.S.-European economic, commercial, and financial ties, the bilateral relationship between the United States and the UK stands out. Despite the asymmetry that characterizes the size of their respective economies (the UK economy in 2004 was roughly 15 percent of its U.S. counterpart), the two countries are important trading partners. The United States was the UK's largest export partner in 2005, accounting for some 15 percent of UK exports. In imports, the United States was the UK's second largest partner at 9.2 percent (behind only Germany).[6] For the United States, the UK is the sixth largest overseas partner in trade in goods. In trade in services, the UK is now competing with the Caribbean financial centers as the largest U.S. trading partner. In two-way tourism, also, the UK is Washington's most important partner. In 2004, the UK accounted for 4.3 percent of total U.S. exports, while imports from the UK that year were 3.1 percent of total U.S. imports.

More significant is the level of cross-investment. The UK is the top destination for U.S. investment, accounting in 2004 for 10 percent of total U.S. worldwide investment and 28 percent of its investment in Europe. The total stock of U.S. investment in the UK, nearly $300 billion, is about 30 percent greater than the second most important destination for U.S. investors — Canada. Thanks to U.S. investment, 1.3 million UK workers go to work each morning; on the other side of the Atlantic, a few hours later, 1.2 Americans go to work generated by investment from the UK.

These levels of interaction in trade and investment are representative samples of a much fuller set of economic and business relations that bind the two countries. Two other areas help define the wider set of relations. The first — the area in which the rubric "special relationship" is perhaps most defensible — is in financial markets, in which both countries are world powers. Is it a surprise, then, that there are more U.S.-owned banks in London than in New York? The second is in defense industry cooperation — the by-product of the strong bilateral and multilateral defense ties between the two countries. This cooperation extends from trade in defense equipment to technology sharing.

In addition, there is the element of economic dynamism. Pause to consider the background of a Europe that has been anemic economically over recent years, with an environment of relatively high unemployment and pervasive workforce rigidities, all in the context of political and social welfare systems that have failed to demonstrate a capacity to adapt to future challenges (such as their aging population and associated financially challenged welfare and retirement systems). Compared with all of this, the UK is truly a bright spot. As Dr. Ray Raymond noted during our deliberations, the UK economy has grown steadily over the past 6 years — pushing it in front of France as the world's fourth largest economy and positioning it to overtake Germany as the third largest, possibly by the year 2012. That economic dynamism, coupled with the similarities between the economic and business systems, suggests that the UK is already a "strategic" partner of the United States and poised to become an even more significant partner in the future.

The contrast between this economic performance and other EU countries is striking. Over the past 2 years, for example, growth in

France has slowed from 2.1 percent to 1.9 percent, and unemployment has risen from 9.0 percent to 10.2 percent; in the Netherlands, the unemployment rate last April was at its highest level in 9 years, while the growth rate has fallen from 1.4 to 1.0 percent.[7] These two countries—two states which rejected by popular referendum the EU constitution this spring—are symptomatic of many other of the EU member states with respect to less than favorable economic prospects. They make the economic dynamism in the UK all the more noteworthy.

For these reasons—a shared "language," a common outlook based on the Anglo-Saxon model, vibrant bilateral trade and investment ties, and economic vitality—there is a solid case that the special relationship carries over to the economic and commercial sphere. To suggest, however, that these elements will allow for the perpetuation of the distinctive nature of the long-term relationship may be premature. As Winston Churchill observed, "It is a mistake to try to look too far ahead. The chain of destiny can only be grasped one link at a time."

How Special?

In the light of the foregoing areas of established cooperation, then, what are the factors that should temper our optimism about the future of the special relationship? The first and most obvious element is London's membership in the EU. That the UK has committed itself to the integration implied by the EU process suggests a number of constraints on how "special" bilateral relations with the United States can be. Despite the fact that the UK and the United States share a number of priorities with respect to international economic and financial policies, ultimately London is bound by its relationship with the EU and the process by which the EU member states seek to effect higher levels of economic and financial integration, *inter alia*. Because the United States and the EU sometimes have conflicting interests and positions, this by definition suggests the possibility that London and Washington may find themselves on the opposite sides of disputes.

As Michael Calingaert described it during our deliberations, by virtue of its EU membership, the UK is "not a free agent in terms of economic policies and actions." The fact is that the UK has conferred competences to Brussels in a number of areas—not least of which are trade and competition policy. It follows that from the standpoint of Washington, Brussels—and not London or the other EU member-state capitals—must be the focus in these broader economic and business interactions.

True, the UK can play an even more significant role in shaping developments within the EU and therefore in U.S.-EU relations. London has played a positive role over the years in many of the trade issues that have surfaced between Washington and Brussels including, for example, chemical substances, the action on the Foreign Sales Corporation, biotech and genetically-modified organisms, and steel imports. Still, a number of bilateral problems persist—including frictions over civil aviation. Another consideration is that London's capacity to influence the course of EU decisionmaking is in itself limited.

The second element overshadowing the special relationship is the ongoing shift in the global economy. The United States must necessarily determine how its relations with the UK compare with the sets of relations that Washington has with other economic powers. As other countries—in particular, Brazil, Russia, India, and China (the "BRIC" countries)—continue to expand rapidly and in the process shift production and consumption patterns and the very balance of the global economy, the United States must also pursue and balance a number of newly "special" relations as it seeks to achieve its broader economic and commercial goals.

There are looming demographic issues, especially in continental Europe, which suggest potential structural constraints in longer-term economic growth. Aging populations in many of the European countries will bring to the surface long-postponed adjustments in retirement and health benefits. Among other things, increasing expenditures on pension and medical care could crowd out public spending on everything from infrastructure to the military. My CSIS colleague, Richard Jackson, has estimated that public pension and health care benefits for the G-7 countries will rise from 5.8 percent of gross domestic product (GDP) in 1960 to 21.7 percent in 2030, leaving little room for other areas of public spending.[8] A key uncertainty, therefore, is whether Europe's freedom of maneuver will become increasingly limited — with the obvious implications that such a reduction suggests for alliance politics between Europe and Washington. That, it turn, has ominous overtones for the future of U.S.-UK relations as well.

Developments on the U.S. side of the Atlantic could also serve to constrain the extent to which relations are authentically special. Adrian Kendry highlighted during our discussions the concern in Europe — and the UK — that the outlook for relations is contingent on broader economic and financial trends in the United States. Not least of these concerns are the "twin deficits" in the United States (the Federal budget as well as trade) and the capacity of the United States to maintain economic dynamism in the face of potential dislocations generated by these imbalances.

Beyond that, there is the potential that widening political positions between the United States and Europe — on the current military operation in Iraq, for example — could spill over into the economic and commercial realms. A number of such issues — ranging from differences on the Middle East to international frameworks such as the Kyoto Protocol — could manifest themselves in a gradual erosion of traditional U.S.-Europe trade and financial ties. This would have an obvious impact on U.S.-UK relations.

Moving Forward.

When these important links between Washington and London and potential future divisions are weighed together, what recommendations materialize? I would point to four.

- The first is to acknowledge that the relationship, even if tempered by uncertainties about the future and qualifications about current directions, is genuinely special, and that perpetuation of this special relationship, as Secretary Straw argued, could indeed be instrumental to achieving a better and safer world. After all, leaders in Washington and London have a very significant common agenda with respect to economic, trade, investment, and commercial issues.

- Second, despite the shifts in world economic powers and the diverse nature of U.S. interests around the world, the UK does indeed represent an important set of bilateral relations with the United States. It is also a key player inside the EU. As such, furthering the special relationship implies the possibility that London could "bridge" issues between the United States and Europe — including trade liberalization, the pursuit of jointly determined interests with third-party states, etc.

- Third, in order to effect such an authentically special relationship, the two sides must redouble efforts to strengthen structural consultations and communication. Although this applies to communication across the board, it is no less important to making progress in a constellation of bilateral economic and commercial issues. In that regard, both sides would be well-served were it possible to emulate the "Zoellick-Lamy" model (based on the prior interaction between then U.S. Trade Representative Robert Zoellick and then EU Trade Commissioner Pascal Lamy) — at both the bilateral level as well as in U.S.-EU relations.

- Finally, it is in the interest of both sides to define a more nearly strategic agenda in the economic and commercial realm and then seek to implement that agenda in the respective national contexts. This implies challenging both sides to engage in a frank assessment of common interests and obstacles, and then to work together to achieve commonly defined objectives.

In the final analysis, the U.S.-UK special relationship transcends the fact that we have a common language and a common outlook. The relationship is special for many more reasons, not least of which is that leaders on both sides have a long-standing commitment to work together on the many international challenges — economic and otherwise — that they confront.

ENDNOTES

1. President George W. Bush, "President Discusses American and European Alliance in Belgium," Concert Noble, Brussels, Belgium, February 21, 2005.

2. "A Trans Atlantic Agenda For the Year Ahead," Remarks by Under Secretary of State for Political Affairs Nicholas Burns, Chatham House, London, April 6, 2005.

3. The *CIA Factbook* suggests that in the year 2004, as measured in purchasing-power-parity terms, the U.S. economy stood at $11.75 trillion and the EU economy

at $11.65 trillion. Together, the two economies accounted for more than 42 percent of global economic output. See *http://www.cia.gov/cia/publications/factbook/*.

4. For a description of the G8's program on African development, see for example the official site of the July 6-8, 2005, G8 meeting at the Gleneagles Summit at Perthshire, Scotland, UK, at *http://www.g8.gov.uk/*. For a description of the G8's program on weapons of mass destruction, see the statement on "The G8 Global Partnership Against the Spread of Weapons and Materials of Mass Destruction," Kananaskis, Canada, June 27, 2002, at *http://www.g7.utoronto.ca/summit/2002kananaskis/arms.html*.

5. See, for example, Harold Brown and Giuliano Amato, "Six Attainable Transatlantic Goals," *The Financial Times*, April 8, 2005, at *http://www.csis.org/europe/050406_SixGoals.pdf*.

6. Data for 2004. *CIA Factbook*, at *http://www.cia.gov/cia/publications/factbook/geos/uk.html#top*.

7. Robin Niblett, "Shock Therapy," *CSIS Euro-Focus*, Vol. 11, No. 2, June 3, 2005, p. 1.

8. Unpublished presentation entitled "The Challenge of Global Aging," June 2005. Jackson bases his projections on Central Intelligence Agency, Organization for Economic Cooperation and Development, and Office of Management and Budget data from various years.

SECTION II:

POLITICAL AND LEGAL ASPECTS
OF THE SPECIAL RELATIONSHIP

CHAPTER 5

THE ANXIETY OF SOVEREIGNTY:
BRITAIN, THE UNITED STATES, AND THE
INTERNATIONAL CRIMINAL COURT

Douglas E. Edlin

INTRODUCTION

The United States and Britain disagree about several legal issues with a political dimension, or political issues with a legal dimension, ranging from landmines to climate change.[1] But unlike disagreements over the Ottawa Convention and the Kyoto Protocol, given both nations' shared cultural, historical, and constitutional commitments to the rule of law and judicial independence as a means of securing fundamental values and governmental accountability, the disagreement between Britain and the United States over the International Criminal Court (ICC) seems especially unexpected. As I will explain in this chapter, though, the nations' divergent positions toward the ICC perhaps are not as surprising as they first appear.

Given the current international political and military mobilization against agents of terrorism around the world, the presence of an international criminal tribunal provides a legal mechanism for prosecuting those who commit terrorist acts (as well as, perhaps, those who might resort to untoward methods while pursuing otherwise legitimate military operations on foreign soil). This chapter examines the development of the ICC, outlines the positions of and disagreements between Britain and the United States concerning it, and analyzes the specific objections to the ICC raised by the United States. In this discussion, I will argue that the contrasting positions of Britain and the United States toward the ICC can be understood in terms of each nation's differently configured perception of its own sovereign power. For various reasons, it seems that Britain's sovereignty is tested most acutely by its relationship with the European Union (EU),[2] while the United States feels its sovereignty is encroached upon primarily by its relationship with the United Nations (UN).[3]

THE ORIGINS AND JURISDICTION
OF THE INTERNATIONAL CRIMINAL COURT

The ICC traces its antecedents back, ultimately, to the Nuremberg Trials.[4] British leaders had grave doubts about the efficacy of an international tribunal; the official British position toward the punishment of identified war criminals from 1943 until the end of the war was summary execution.[5] Nevertheless, Nuremberg and the aftermath of World War II generated international awareness of and momentum for the creation of an international legal tribunal responsible for the prosecution and punishment of those responsible for war crimes.[6] After Nuremberg, and in light of persistent questions about the legal legitimacy of those proceedings,[7] the UN General Assembly appointed a body of experts to organize and codify international legal principles. In particular, this International Law Commission (ILC) was asked to draft a statute instituting an international criminal court along with an international criminal code, the so-called "Nuremberg Principles," which would be enforced by the international criminal tribunal.[8]

These efforts culminated in the ILC's draft statute for the creation of an international criminal court in 1994. Two years later, the ILC completed its draft international criminal code. As background to the ILC's work, international pressure was building for the creation of tribunals to try individuals in connection with the human rights atrocities in the former Yugoslavia. In 1994 the UN Security Council passed a resolution to create a second ad hoc tribunal as a result of the genocidal activities in Rwanda.[9]

Building on the ILC's draft statute and referencing the two ad hoc tribunals as prototypes, the UN General Assembly issued resolutions that led to the Diplomatic Conference of Plenipotentiaries on the Establishment of an International Criminal Court, which met in Rome beginning on June 15, 1998. On July 17, the Rome Statute of the International Criminal Court was signed by 120 states, with 21 abstentions and over the objections of seven states, including the United States.[10] The ICC was formally created upon the ratification of the Rome Statute by 60 states and entered into force on July 1, 2002.

Four crimes may be prosecuted before the ICC: genocide, crimes against humanity, war crimes, and aggression.[11] These crimes are understood to possess an intrinsic international dimension as a result of their scope and extraordinary inhumanity, which raise a concern for all nations. The jurisdictional limitation of the ICC to these four crimes is tied to its historical predecessor at Nuremberg, because all four of these crimes also were prosecuted in some form at the Nuremberg Trials.[12] Also, like Nuremberg, the ICC was created to provide a forum for prosecution of leaders and organizers most responsible for these crimes, not lower-level functionaries.[13] Indeed, the Rome Statute specifically rejects official capacity as a bar to prosecution and highlights the potential criminal responsibility of commanders and other superiors.[14] At the same time, the ICC hearkens back to Nuremberg by expressly precluding exculpation for core crimes through the defense that those responsible were "just following orders."[15] Finally, the ICC contains explicit provisions that preclude the legal and theoretical challenges raised concerning the legitimacy of Nuremberg. By specific, separate articles, the ICC incorporates the principles of *nullum crimen sine lege, nulla poena sine lege*, and a prohibition against *ex post facto* criminalization.[16]

The ICC is most sharply distinguished from its predecessor tribunals by its jurisdictional mandate. Unlike the Nuremberg tribunal and the Yugoslav and Rwandan ad hoc tribunals,[17] the ICC's jurisdiction is consensual and complementary. In other words, the states that consented to the jurisdiction of the ICC also consented to permit prosecutions in a supranational court of crimes committed on their soil or by their citizens. However, the ICC's jurisdiction only complements or supplements the authority of a state's national courts. The ICC assumes jurisdiction over trials for the four core crimes when, and only when, the national judiciary of the state in question is unwilling or unable to proceed.[18]

BRITISH AND AMERICAN POSITIONS REGARDING THE ICC

Britain's support was pivotal to the creation of the ICC, beginning with the formative discussions in 1997 of the Preparatory Committee on the Creation of an International Criminal Court (PrepCom). At the

December 1997 PrepCom meeting, Britain agreed to withdraw the demand that ICC proceedings would depend upon prior Security Council approval. This "dramatic shift" altered the course of the negotiations and was a departure from the American position,[19] although the issue of prior referral by suitable authority would return and remain contentious in Rome.[20] In addition, in contrast to other Security Council members, Britain joined the so-called "like-minded group" (LMG) of smaller and mid-level states that wished the ICC to be a strong, influential court.[21] Britain signed the Rome Statute on November 30, 1998, and ratified the Statute on October 4, 2001.[22]

As the varying and contradictory U.S. formal postures indicate, American attitudes toward the ICC have been decidedly ambivalent. This ambivalence is further demonstrated by the U.S. decision to vote against the Rome Statute when it was initially adopted in Rome on July 17, 1998. The United States then chose to sign the Rome Statute on the final day it remained open for signature, December 31, 2000. The United States then reversed its position again and "unsigned" the Rome Statute on May 6, 2002.[23]

The United States followed its repudiation of the ICC with the enactment by Congress of the American Servicemembers' Protection Act (ASPA), which ensures (so far as U.S. domestic law and policy are concerned) that no American soldier or government official will be subject to ICC jurisdiction.[24] In fact, Section 7423 of ASPA specifically precludes any American court, state entity, or agency from supporting or assisting the ICC, and prevents any agent of the ICC from conducting any investigative activity on American territory.[25] Where American and allied forces conduct joint operations in which an American is under the command of a state party national, ASPA authorizes the President to attempt to reduce the risk of American exposure to ICC jurisdiction.[26] As a preemptive tactic, the United States has entered into bilateral agreements with dozens of nations in an effort to guarantee that these nations will never refer any American for prosecution before the ICC and has conditioned American participation in multinational military operations upon international immunization from ICC prosecution.[27]

U.S. OBJECTIONS TO THE ICC

American reluctance to join the ICC might seem peculiar, given that the ICC was originally an American idea.[28] The ICC has been accepted by the other allied nations and Security Council members that formed the Nuremberg tribunal (Britain, France, and Russia), every NATO nation (except Turkey), and Mexico. Nevertheless, the ICC was perceived by certain influential government officials as a "threat to American sovereignty and international freedom of action."[29] This perceived threat related, at least according to these officials, to the prospect of the ICC restricting the United States (regardless of whether the United States subjected itself to ICC jurisdiction) from pursuing certain forceful responses to acts of aggression out of fear of prosecution before the ICC. As these officials put it, "The last thing America's leaders need is an additional reason not to respond when our nation's interests are threatened."[30]

American objections to the ICC all stem, in one form or another, from perceived threats to United States sovereignty.[31] At hearings on the ICC held one week after the Rome Conference, Senator Rod Grams stated to the Senate Foreign Relations Committee that "the United States will not cede its sovereignty to an institution which claims to have the power to override the U.S. legal system and pass judgment on our foreign policy actions," and Senator Larry Craig claimed that the ICC represented "a fundamental threat to American sovereignty."[32] Such rhetoric demands, but sometimes overwhelms, careful examination of the concerns the ICC raises for the United States. In an effort to clarify and analyze these concerns, I will organize America's objections to the ICC into six distinct but overlapping categories: institutional, constitutional, doctrinal, security, prosecution, and symbolic.

Institutional Objections.

Institutionally, the ICC is viewed by some as supplanting the UN Security Council. According to the UN Charter, the Security Council has "primary responsibility for the maintenance of international peace and security . . ." and provides the Council with power to "determine the existence of any threat to the peace, breach of the peace, or act of agression and . . . [to] decide what measures shall be taken. . . ."[33] The ICC, at least arguably, frustrates the UN Charter by usurping this role from the Security Council and by depriving the United States of its veto of Security Council measures. Accordingly, the United States (and others) sought prior review by the Security Council as a precondition for ICC proceedings. Absent a prior Security Council *imprimatur*, action by the ICC strikes some as displacing the role of the Security Council and nullifying the effect of the UN Charter.[34] Of course, the response to this point is that the requirement of Security Council permission prior to ICC action effectively would negate any authority the ICC could have as an independent tribunal, particularly where an investigation or prosecution of a Security Council member or its allies was deemed necessary.

Constitutional Objections.

The ICC does not offer criminal procedures and protections that coincide completely with those offered under the U.S. Constitution. Most obviously, the ICC trial of an American need not (and would not) take place in "the State and district wherein the crime shall have been committed."[35] Moreover, the ICC has no jury trial provision[36] and does not protect against unreasonable searches and seizures, although it does acknowledge a modified form of exclusionary rule for improperly obtained evidence.[37] Despite the presence of many familiar, fundamental constitutional protections afforded to criminal defendants under the U.S. Constitution and traditional American criminal procedure—such as *Miranda* warnings, presumption of innocence, notice of charges, assistance of counsel, prompt and public trial, modified confrontation and compulsory process, privilege against self-incrimination, and double jeopardy[38]—the ICC does not protect Americans to the same degree that the U.S. Constitution does.

Another constitutional objection to the ICC concerns the legal source of its judicial authority. If we imagine that the U.S. Senate ratified the Rome Statute, it might seem that the ICC is just another court, which Congress has chosen to accept through its Article II advice and consent power[39] rather than to create through its Article III power.[40] The problem is that Article III of the Constitution vests U.S. judicial power "in one supreme Court" and grants Congress the power to ordain and establish "inferior Courts." Joining the Rome Statute would give the ICC jurisdiction over American citizens for acts committed on American soil. Given the theoretical possibility that the ICC could prosecute an American for a crime committed in the United States and that the ICC's decision could not be reviewed by the U.S. Supreme Court, the ICC would be exercising U.S. judicial authority in a manner not contemplated or tolerated by the Constitution.[41] Under these circumstances, the ICC genuinely could not be considered an "inferior court" and the ICC's recognition as a judicial authority over American citizens by the U.S. government would seem to conflict with the constitutional mandate that there be "one Supreme Court." Granting the ICC judicial authority over American nationals in a manner consistent with the U.S. Constitution would seem to require a constitutional amendment rather than a treaty. The need for a constitutional amendment prior to American acceptance of the ICC underscores the advantage (or the disadvantage) of having a written constitution.

Doctrinal Objections.

A central U.S. concern involves the ICC provision granting it jurisdiction over nationals of nonparty states who are accused of crimes committed on the territory of party states.[42] According to settled and fundamental doctrines of international law, a treaty is binding only upon the parties that sign and ratify it (unless the treaty codifies general customary international law principles).[43] The subjection of nonparties to ICC jurisdiction seems to conflict with this fundamental doctrine.[44]

There are three related responses to this objection. First, American resistance to the existence of the ICC or to American participation in the ICC could not prevent Americans from being tried by a foreign tribunal if, for example, members of the American military carrying out operations on foreign soil were accused of one of the crimes within the jurisdiction of the ICC (i.e., genocide, crimes against humanity, war crimes, or aggression). On the contrary, American military personnel who found themselves in this situation would, according to principles of international law, be subject to the jurisdiction of the courts of the state in which the operations were conducted.[45] Second, and related to the previous point, the ICC's jurisdictional mandate simply incorporates the traditional jurisdictional foundations of nationality and territoriality. In other words, Article 12 of the Rome Statute merely allows the ICC to do what national judiciaries commonly do, *viz.*, exercise jurisdiction over their own nationals for crimes committed outside state borders and exercise jurisdiction over nationals from other states who commit crimes within the subject state's territory. Third, the United States has ratified several treaties that require prosecution by state parties of any individual suspected of defined criminal activity, even if the accused's home country has not ratified the treaty. These treaties apparently conflict with the notion that a treaty cannot authorize jurisdiction over nonparties. Certainly this notion has not prevented the United States from executing these treaties.[46] Such inconsistency raises doubts about the gravity of American objections to the ICC grounded on its purported violation of fundamental principles of international law.

Security Objections.

In a manner related to ICC jurisdiction over nonparties, the United States argued in Rome and subsequently maintained that this unprecedented extension of international jurisdiction could restrict significantly military operations necessary to preserve American national security or to restore or maintain peace in politically volatile regions. For example, the United States maintains a wide-ranging commitment to employ its forces in peacekeeping missions around the world. This, it is argued, raises a not unlikely possibility:

> American servicemen on duty in the 1990-91 Persian Gulf conflict or in the operations in Somalia would be subject to frivolous charges raised in the [International Criminal] Court by Iraqi President Saddam Hussein or Somali leader General Aidid solely to deflect international criticism from their own egregious behavior. Then, in order to avoid the possibility of "malicious prosecution" of this nature, the U.S. reduces its commitment to participate in crucial international peacekeeping missions, thereby

increasing the risk of global instability and war. In particular, this jurisdictional element has led to the United States seeking and securing immunization from ICC prosecution prior to committing troops for international peacekeeping missions.[47]

These concerns are raised not only by politicians and others who oppose any form of international influence on U.S. policymaking. The concern about the threat of malicious prosecutions inhibiting U.S. participation in international peacekeeping missions is considered significant even by Ambassador David Scheffer, who headed the American delegation at the Rome conference.[48]

Prosecution Objections.

A concern closely related to the previous discussion addresses the possibility that the ICC might be used to pursue political agendas rather than war criminals. The United States sees itself as a likely target for politically-motivated prosecutions before the ICC and therefore is reluctant to support the creation of a tribunal that might be manipulated pursuant to such political motivations. Additionally, America objects to the authority of the ICC prosecutor to initiate an investigation even in the absence of any state party or Security Council complaint or referral.[49] For many U.S. military members, this is the insurmountable obstacle to America signing the Rome Statute or complying with the ICC. As Lieutenant Colonel William Lietzau puts it:

> Because the jurisdictional regime does not adequately protect U.S. troops and commanders from politically motivated prosecutions, the United States cannot sign the treaty . . . . [T]he Rome negotiators settled on a regime that fell short of U.S. objectives to maintain certain jurisdictional control over its own forces. . . . Referrals initiating such [ICC] jurisdiction can derive from any of three sources: the UN Security Council, a state party to the Statute, or the prosecutor acting in his or her independent capacity. The U.S. military has been much criticized for its stance on this critical aspect of the ICC Statute, but what the critics sometimes fail to recognize are the unique and vital national security responsibilities of the U.S. armed forces and the consequences of their front-line role in carrying out the nation's national security strategy. . . . [N]o other state regularly has nearly 200,000 troops outside its borders, either forward deployed or

engaged in one of several operations designed to preserve international peace and security. . . . Soldiers deployed far from home need to do their jobs without exposure to politicized proceedings.[50]

However, other American military personnel, such as Major General William Nash (Retired), point out that few foreign nations have accepted American assertions of exemption from ICC jurisdiction. So in the event that an ICC investigation or prosecution required compliance by foreign states or actors, American opposition to the ICC is unlikely to have much effect.[51] Moreover, the military might have an interest in supporting the ICC, because American forces serving overseas are at the greatest risk of becoming victims of war crimes. So it could be in the interest of the military to see war crimes investigated, prosecuted, and punished as extensively and vigorously as possible.[52]

Symbolic Objections.

The final, and in some ways the most fundamental, U.S. objection to the ICC is captured by the imagined spectacle of an American president or high-ranking military or political official standing trial before a non-American tribunal. The ICC does not recognize claims of official immunity,[53] and it is unclear whether the ICC would honor a national grant of amnesty that shielded individuals from ICC prosecution. Accordingly, the concern about the spectacle and its symbolic and practical effects on American position, prestige, and power is not merely hypothetical. Its very possibility is intolerable to the sensibilities of many Americans. Of course, the response to this objection is that the prospective national embarrassment of a leader being prosecuted before the ICC would itself be a salutary deterrent effect of the tribunal's existence. This is hardly a basis for American objections to the ICC.

NATIONAL SOVEREIGNTY IN A GLOBAL COMMUNITY

One plausible explanation for the disparate British and U.S. reactions toward the ICC might be found in their reactions to the perceived sovereignty threats posed by the EU and the UN, respectively. Britain has, after some constitutional indigestion, accepted the supremacy of EU law in two judicially relevant ways. First, Britain accepts—as all EU members ultimately must—the supranational jurisdiction of the European Court of Justice (ECJ) and the European Court of Human Rights (ECHR). Given that British citizens and the British government may appear as parties before the ECJ and the ECHR, and that the decisions of those courts are binding upon Britain's national judiciary, Britain has acknowledged the judicial authority over its citizens of courts outside its borders. Second, EU law is directly enforceable by the national courts of Britain. British courts therefore apply external legal doctrine that has been incorporated into British law through, for example, the Human Rights Act of 1998.[54] As a result of these two factors, by virtue of which Britain has made its (sometimes uneasy) peace with its presence within the EU, it likely does not view the ICC as a radical challenge to the authority or autonomy of its governmental structure.

Unlike Britain and the EU, influential elements of the U.S. government continue to view the UN with measured circumspection. The United States tends to be most supportive of UN action when that action has no direct repercussions on U.S. foreign policy. Moreover, Americans tend to view their courts and their law as entirely sufficient for the expression and maintenance of legal doctrine and government accountability. Indeed, Supreme Court justices still have serious reservations about citing, to say nothing of following, decisions of foreign courts such as the ECHR.[55]

In other words, there is a constitutional dimension to sovereignty itself, which some would say American subjection to the ICC would contravene. The unwritten British constitution is generally understood to grant Parliament the unfettered authority to bind Britain and its subjects to supranational jurisdiction as a condition of its constitutional authority. As with the EU, the power of Parliament to submit Britain to the ICC is a demonstration of Parliament's constitutional sovereignty. Unlike the case of the British Parliament, however, the very act of subjecting an American citizen to ICC jurisdiction might be a violation of America's constitutional authority in the absence of a constitutional amendment. Without amending the Constitution, some Americans would claim that deference to the ICC is tantamount to the abandonment of republican self-government.[56] According to this view, the mere existence of the ICC (should the United States ever join it) would constitute a challenge to American constitutional democracy, because for the first time in U.S. history, an institution outside the U.S. government would have "the ultimate authority to judge the policies adopted and implemented by the elected officials of the United States—the core attribute of sovereignty and the *sine qua non* of democratic self-government."[57]

Nevertheless, it seems entirely plausible that American republican government permits Congress to commit the United States, on behalf of the people, to an international or supranational institution with genuine influence over U.S. policy. There is nothing inherently undemocratic about giving governmental representatives the authority to bind their constituencies in ways that the constituents find surprising or objectionable. To borrow a phrase from the British context, so long as this congressional authority is not viewed as "self-embracing," there is no threat to American sovereignty or democracy, because not all delegations of sovereignty are derogations of sovereignty. Indeed, some would say it is the essence of constitutional democracy that the majority's representatives may take certain actions to preserve and promote constitutional values, fundamental rights, and the rule of law, despite the majority's disapproval.[58]

Notwithstanding these differing perceptions of their place in the international community, the Anglo-American commitment to the rule of law both within and beyond national borders offers a meaningful incentive to support an international court of criminal justice. In the end, as Gary Bass explains, "[A] war crimes tribunal is an extension of the rule of law from the domestic sphere to the international sphere. . . . [T]he serious pursuit of international justice rests on principled legalist beliefs held by only a few liberal governments."[59]

Britain and the United States are two of these few liberal governments. Britain's preference for summary execution of war criminals rather than legalism after World War II was the sole aberration in the commitment of liberal states to legalism when confronting war crimes.[60] The rejection of the ICC by the United States is now, arguably, the second. The Anglo-American commitment to the rule of law and the historical contribution of both nations to the development of due process and norms of justice enforced by an independent judiciary has, in the past, anchored a shared commitment to legalism in the pursuit of international justice.[61] Britain and America have supported international war crimes tribunals largely out of a belief in the fundamental fairness of their own tradition of constitutional protection of criminal defendants and the intrinsic value of their principles and process as a means of achieving justice domestically and internationally.[62] At Nuremberg, the United States had to persuade (or remind) Britain that trials alone were the only means of achieving justice for war crimes consistent with Anglo-American legalism.[63] Perhaps Britain needs to return the favor with respect to the ICC. Though, to be fair, the United States strongly supports an international court of criminal justice (but not one that would try Americans without American consent).

Inasmuch as Anglo-American dedication to international norms of justice enforced by international tribunals derives, at least in part, from the recognition and reinforcement of domestic rule of law values in those international norms and tribunals, it is reasonable to see Anglo-American legalism itself as a manifestation of national sovereignty. After all, "sovereignty does not arise in a vacuum, but is constituted by the recognition of the international community, which makes its recognition conditional on certain standards. . . ."[64] Just as American democracy theoretically is predicated upon a relinquishment of a measure of liberty in exchange for security and individual autonomy in a larger social context, so too can support for the ICC be viewed as the relinquishment of a measure of sovereignty in exchange for security and international respect in a global context. Put differently, supporting the ICC does not just mean sacrificing sovereignty, it also enhances sovereignty.[65]

To be sure, this view of sovereignty depends upon a particular view of the nature of political power. Power, in this view, is more than the ability of one state to bend other states to its will through coercion; it is also the ability of one state to persuade other states that their interests align. In other words, soft power can, in certain circumstances, be more effective than hard power.[66] If the United

States will achieve more, including the achievement of more of its own political goals, in a world that respects American leadership, then its ongoing opposition to the ICC may engender a very real loss of American influence and, ultimately, of American sovereignty and security.[67] The international perception that U.S. opposition to the ICC tarnishes the long-standing American commitment to the rule of law inside and outside its borders could limit America's ability to influence international affairs and thus ultimately detract from America's sovereignty.[68]

CONCLUSION

U.S. rejection of the ICC has angered U.S. allies, increased resentment toward the United States around the world, raised doubts about American commitments to the preservation of the rule of law nationally and internationally, and seemingly distanced the United States from the nation otherwise most closely associated with American values of legalism and support of norms and institutions of international justice. All of these factors inevitably lead one to wonder whether the current U.S. position toward the ICC is prudent politically. Some commentators suggest that a less unilateral position toward the ICC would serve American interests for four reasons: (1) the practical risk of prosecution of American citizens before the ICC is extremely remote;[69] (2) American negotiating influence would not be weakened in contexts such as the Security Council, where U.S. rejection of the ICC, among other things, led to international reluctance to support American military intervention in Iraq;[70] (3) the current U.S. policy has floundered because of the backlash against bilateral agreements immunizing Americans against future referral for ICC prosecution, the refusal of most significant powers to sign them, and the U.S. inability to alter the fundamental structure of the ICC or to influence policy relative to the ICC now that the United States is no longer a party to the Rome Statute;[71] and (4) the apparent inconsistency between America's commitment to rule of law values and its unwillingness to comply with the ICC as an institution dedicated to the preservation of human rights through international legal norms has eroded America's political and moral capital as a leader in international affairs.[72]

Our friends influence our decisions even, or especially, when we disagree with them. Just as Britain's acceptance of the Ottawa Convention influenced America's decision not to employ landmines during joint military operations in Afghanistan after September 11, 2001,[73] so too can Britain's decision to join the ICC influence American actions during joint military operations. To the extent that the very existence of the ICC promotes a "culture of accountability,"[74] the ICC may exert an influence over American policy even if Americans are never subject to ICC jurisdiction. Of course, this influence on American policy will strike those Americans who oppose the ICC as validation of their initial concerns, and this influence will strike American supporters of the ICC as mitigation of their misgivings over U.S. withdrawal from the ICC. In the end, the ICC raises the question of whether constitutionalism is a domestic or a universal concept.[75] In other words, the ICC tests the Anglo-American commitment to the rule of law, in part by asking what law will rule. Britain and the United States share a cultural, historical, theoretical, and doctrinal commitment to the rule of law, and this commitment has grounded Anglo-American support for international war crimes tribunals in the past. But Britain seems more willing than the United States to accept that, at least where the ICC is concerned, the law that will rule Britain and its leaders and citizens can sometimes be made by an institution beyond its borders, while the United States remains committed to the rule of law solely as defined and limited by U.S. law.

CHAPTER 5 - ENDNOTES

1. See, e.g., *Convention on the Prohibition of the Use, Stockpiling, Production and Transfer of Anti-Personnel Mines and on Their Destruction*, September 18, 1997, 36 I.L.M. 1507 (the Ottawa Convention, ratified by Britain but not by the United States); *The Kyoto Protocol to the United Nations Framework Convention on Climate Change*, December 11, 1997, early draft reprinted at 37 I.L.M. 22 (the Kyoto Protocol, ratified by Britain but not by the United States).

2. See, generally, Paul Craig, "Britain in the European Union," in Jeffrey Jowell and Dawn Oliver, eds., *The Changing Constitution* (4th ed.), Oxford University Press, 2000, especially pp. 69-79. See also *Rv Secretary of State for Transport, ex parte Factortame Ltd. (No. 2)* [1991] 1 AC 603; Danny Nicol, *EC Membership and the Judicialization of British Politics*, Oxford University Press, 2000, ch. 7.

3. See, e.g., Representative Bob Barr, "Protecting National Sovereignty in an Era of International Meddling: An Increasingly Difficult Task," *Harvard Journal on Legislation*, Vol. 39, 2002, pp. 299, 308 ("[T]he United Nations' attempts to institutionalize intrusions into United States decision-making present a threat every bit as real to United States sovereignty as was posed previously by the Soviet Union"); Winston P. Nagan, "Strengthening Humanitarian Law: Sovereignty, International Criminal Law and the Ad Hoc Tribunal for the Former Yugoslavia," *Duke Journal of Comparative and International Law*, Vol. 6, 1995, pp. 127, 138, n.46.

4. See, generally, Andrew Clapham, "Issues of Complexity, Complicity and Complementarity: From the Nuremberg Trials to the Dawn of the New International Criminal Court," in Philippe Sands, ed., *From Nuremberg to The Hague: The Future of International Criminal Justice*, Cambridge University Press, 2003, ch. 2; Marcella David, "Grotius Repudiated: The American Objections to the International Criminal Court and the Commitment to International Law," *Michigan Journal of International Law*, Vol. 20, 1999, pp. 337, 346-354.

5. See Richard Overy, "The Nuremberg Trials: International Law in the Making," in Philippe Sands, ed., *From Nuremberg to The Hague: The Future of International Criminal Justice*, Cambridge University Press, 2003, pp. 3-4.

6. See, generally, Gary Jonathan Bass, *Stay the Hand of Vengeance: The Politics of War Crimes Tribunals*, Princeton University Press, 2000, pp. 149-173.

7. See, generally, Judith N. Shklar, *Legalism: Law, Morals, and Political Trials*, Harvard University Press, 1964, pp. 155-179.

8. See William A. Schabas, *An Introduction to the International Criminal Court*, 2nd ed., Cambridge University Press, 2004, p. 8.

9. *Ibid.*, p. 11.

10. Rome Statute of the International Criminal Court, July 17, 1998, 37 I.L.M. 999 (hereafter, the Rome Statute).

11. Interestingly, there was overwhelming support for including the first three crimes within the ICC's jurisdiction. The crime of aggression ultimately was included "despite the knowledge that no agreement could be reached at the [Rome] conference either on its definition or on the role of the Security Council . . ." Mahnoush H. Arsanjani, "The Rome Statute of the International Criminal Court," *American Journal of International Law*, Vol. 93, 1999, pp. 22, 30.

12. See Schabas, *An Introduction to the International Criminal Court*, pp. 26-27.

13. *Ibid.*, p. 29.

14. *Ibid.*, Articles 27-28.

15. *Ibid.*, Article 33.

16. *Ibid.*, Articles 11, 22-24.

17. See Arsanjani, *The Rome Statute of the International Criminal Court*, Vol. 24, n.13.

18. See Rome Statute, Article 17(1)(a). The conditional nature of ICC jurisdiction is referred to as "complementarity" or "admissibility." See, generally, Schabas, "An Introduction to the International Criminal Court," p. 68; Arsanjani, "The Rome Statute of the International Criminal Court," pp. 24-25, 27-28.

19. See Bartram S. Brown, "Primacy or Complementarity: Reconciling the Jurisdiction of National Courts and International Criminal Tribunals," *Yale Journal of International Law*, 1998, Vol. 23, pp. 383, 429, n.225. The United States believed that prosecution before the ICC should be predicated upon a referral by the Security Council or a state party to the treaty. See David J. Scheffer, "The United States and the International Criminal Court," *American Journal of International Law*, Vol. 93, 1999, pp. 12, 15.

20. See Philippe Kirsch and John T. Holmes, "The Rome Conference on an International Criminal Court: The Negotiating Process," *American Journal of International Law*, 1999, Vol. 93, pp. 2, 8. In the end, referral was maintained in the Statute. ICC jurisdiction depends upon a referral from the Security Council, a state party or the ICC independent prosecutor. See Rome Statute, Article 13.

21. Kirsch and Holmes, "The Rome Conference on an International Criminal Court," p. 4; Arsanjani, "The Rome Statute of the International Criminal Court," p. 23.

22. See Schabas, "An Introduction to the International Criminal Court," p. 419.

23. See T. Alexander Aleinikoff, "Thinking Outside the Sovereignty Box: Transnational Law and the U.S. Constitution," *Texas Law Review*, Vol. 82, 1989, 2000, 2004.

24. American Servicemembers' Protection Act, 22 U.S.C. Sections 7401-7433, 2003.

25. 22 U.S.C. Sections 7423(b) and 7423(h).

26. See Lilian V. Faulhaber, "Recent Development: American Servicemembers' Protection Act of 2002," *Harvard Journal on Legislation*, Vol. 40, 2003, pp. 537, 546.

27. See Security Council Resolution 1497, U.N. SCOR, 58th Session, 4803rd Meeting, 2003. See also Sean D. Murphy, "Efforts to Obtain Immunity from ICC for U.S. Peacekeepers," *American Journal of International Law*, Vol. 96, 2002, pp. 725.

28. See, e.g., Michael A. Newton, "Should the United States Join the International Criminal Court?" *University of California at Davis Journal of International Law and Policy*, Vol. 9, 2002, pp. 35, 38.

29. Letter from Lawrence S. Eagleburger to Rep. Tom DeLay, November 29, 2000, quoted in Arthur W. Rovine, "Memorandum to Congress on the ICC from Current and Past Presidents of the ASIL," *American Journal of International Law*, Vol. 95, 2001, pp. 967, 967.

30. Rovine, "Memorandum to Congress on the ICC," quoting letter from *ibid.*, p. 967.

31. See Bruce Broomhall, *International Justice and the International Criminal Court: Between Sovereignty and the Rule of Law*, Oxford University Press, 2003, p. 165.

32. Quoted in Diane Marie Amann and M. N. S. Sellers, "American Law in a Time of Global Interdependence: The United States of America and the International Criminal Court," *American Journal of Comparative Law*, Vol. 50, 2002, pp. 381, 385, 386.

33. U.N. Charter, Articles 24(1) and 39.

34. See, generally, Amann and Sellers, p. 387.

35. U.S. Constitution, Amendment VI. Cf. Rome Statute, Articles 3(1) 62.

36. See *ibid.*, Articles 39(2)(b)(ii) 74.

37. See *ibid.*, Article 69(7).

38. See *ibid.*, Articles 20, 55(2) 63, 66, 67.

39. U.S. Constitution, Article II, Section 2, clause 2, "He [the President] shall have Power, by and with the Advice and Consent of the Senate to make Treaties . . . ."

40. *Ibid.*, Article III, Section 1.

41. See Casey, *The Case Against the International Criminal Court*, pp. 841-842.

42. See Rome Statute, Article 12.

43. See, e.g., Vienna Convention on the Law of Treaties, May 23, 1969, Articles 34-38, 8 I.L.M. 693, 1155 U.N.T.S. 331 (hereafter the Vienna Convention). This is sometimes expressed through the maxims of *pacta tertiis* (*pacta tertiis nec nocent nec prosunt*) or *pacta sunt servanda*. Ironically, the United States has signed but not ratified the Vienna Convention. See, e.g., *United States v. Yousef*, 327 F.3d 56, 94 n.28, 2d Cir. 2003. This could be understood as U.S. refusal to accept the principle that a treaty binds only its signatories, which would weaken American objections to the Rome Statute based upon this doctrinal principle. See endnote 53 and accompanying text.

44. See Scheffer, "The United States and the International Criminal Court," p. 18.

45. Rovine, Memorandum to Congress on the ICC," pp. 967-968.

46. See Diane F. Orentlicher, "Unilateral Multilateralism: United States Policy Toward the International Criminal Court," *Cornell International Law Journal*, Vol. 36, 2004, pp. 415, 420.

47. David, "Grotius Repudiated," p. 357, footnote deleted.

48. See Scheffer, "The United States and the International Criminal Court," p. 19:

Equally troubling are the implications of Article 12 for the future willingness of the United States and other governments to take significant risks to intervene in foreign lands in order to save human lives or to restore international or regional peace and security. The illogical consequence imposed by Article 12, particularly for nonparties to the treaty, will be to limit severely those lawful, but highly controversial and inherently risky, interventions that the advocates of human rights and world peace so desperately seek from the United States and other military powers. There will be significant new legal and political risks in such interventions, which up to this point have been mostly shielded from politically motivated charges.

See also William K. Lietzau, "International Criminal Law After Rome: Concerns From a U.S. Military Perspective," *Law and Contemporary Problems*, Vol. 64, 2001, pp. 119, 125: "The Rome Treaty will become the single most effective brake on international and regional peacekeeping in the 21st century" (quoting Ambassador Scheffer's testimony before the Senate Foreign Relations Committee).

49. See David, "Grotius Repudiated," p. 356, n.71.

50. Lietzau, "Concerns From a U.S. Military Perspective," pp. 125-126. See also Scheffer, "The United States and the International Criminal Court," p. 18.

51. See William L. Nash, "The ICC and the Deployment of U.S. Armed Forces," in Sewall and Kaysen, "The United States and the International Criminal Court," p. 163.

52. See Bass, *Stay the Hand of Vengeance*, pp. 282-283.

53. See Rome Statute, Article 27.

54. See Craig, "Britain in the European Union," pp. 86-87.

55. See, e.g., *Lawrence v. Texas*, 539 U.S. 558, 598, 2003 (Scalia, J., dissenting); *Knight v. Florida*, 528 U.S. 990, 990, 1999 (Thomas, J., concurring). See also Vicki C. Jackson, "Ambivalent Resistance and Comparative Constitutionalism: Opening Up the Conversation on 'Proportionality,' Rights and Federalism," *University of Pennsylvania Journal of Constitutional Law*, Vol. 1, 1999, p. 583; Mark Tushnet, "Returning with Interest: Observations on Some Putative Benefits of Studying Comparative Constitutional Law," *University of Pennsylvania Journal of Constitutional Law*, Vol. 1, 1998, 325. Cf. *Atkins v. Virginia*, 536 U.S. 304, 316 n.21, 2002, pp. 324-325 (Scalia, J., and Rehnquist, C. J., dissenting); *Printz v. United States*, 521 U.S. 898, 921 n.11, 1997.

56. See Amann and Sellers, "American Law in a Time of Global Interdependence," pp. 400-402.

57. Lee A. Casey, "The Case Against the International Criminal Court," *Fordham International Law Journal*, Vol. 25, 2002, pp. 840, 843-844.

58. See, e.g., Ronald Dworkin, *Freedom's Law: The Moral Reading of the American Constitution*, Harvard University Press, 1996, pp. 15-26.

59. Bass, *Stay the Hand of Vengeance*, pp. 7-8.

60. See above at note 5. See also *ibid.*, pp. 147, 181.

61. *Ibid.*, pp. 148-149, 281.

62. *Ibid.*, p. 173: "At the end of America's most brutal war ever, the Germans would be accorded the benefit of legal procedure as it had evolved in America, because of an American belief in the rightness of its own domestic legalism"; p. 181: "Britain would extend its domestic standards of due process to almost all German war criminals . . . ."

63. *Ibid.*, pp. 150, 180-182.

64. Broomhall, "International Justice and the International Criminal Court," p. 43.

65. *Ibid.*, p. 59.

66. See, e.g., Orentlicher, "Unilateral Multilateralism," pp. 430-431.

67. See, generally, Colonel M. Tia Johnson, "The American Servicemembers' Protection Act: Protecting Whom?" *Virginia Journal of International Law*, Vol. 43, 2003, p. 405.

68. A further point that I cannot develop here is that the concept of sovereignty itself is fundamentally incompatible with the enforcement of international law and should be abandoned. See, e.g., Thomas M. Franck and Stephen H. Yuhan, "The United States and the International Criminal Court: Unilateralism Rampant," *New York University Journal of International Law and Politics*, Vol. 35, 2003, p. 519; Anthony D'Amato, "Human Rights as Part of Customary International Law: A Plea for Change of Paradigms," *Georgia Journal of International and Comparative Law*, Vol. 25, 1995/1996, p. 47.

69. See, e.g., Nash, "The ICC and the Deployment of U.S. Armed Forces," in Sewall and Kaysen, *The United States and the International Criminal Court*, pp. 153, 159.

70. See, e.g., Harold Hongju Koh, "Transnational Legal Process After September 11th," *Berkeley Journal of International Law*, Vol. 22, 2004, pp. 337, 348; Orentlicher, "Unilateral Multilateralism," pp. 428-429. Of course, two of the other actions that increased international animosity toward the United States were its recantation of the Kyoto Protocol and its rejection of the Ottawa Convention. See Orentlicher, "Unilateral Multilateralism," p. 428.

71. See Broomhall, "International Justice and the International Criminal Court," p. 182; Orentlicher, "Unilateral Multilateralism," pp. 430-431, 432: "It can hardly be doubted that the ICC is more likely to operate in accordance with America's vision of the Court if the United States participates in shaping the institution than if it declares open war against it."

72. Cf. Koh, *Transnational Legal Process After September 11th*, 348: "[B]y rejecting a legal process approach, it [the United States] limited itself to coercive solutions, which have now ironically diminished its capacity for global leadership under a banner of rule of law."

73. See Lesley Wexler, "The International Deployment of Shame, Second-Best Responses, and Norm Entrepreneurship: The Campaign to Ban Landmines and the Landmine Ban Treaty," *Arizona Journal of International and Comparative Law*, Vol. 20, 2003, pp. 561, 598.

74. Broomhall, "International Justice and the International Criminal Court," p. 3.

75. Cf. Jed Rubenfeld, "Unilateralism and Constitutionalism," *New York University Law Review*, Vol. 79, 1971, 1991-99, 2004; Casey, "The Case Against the International Criminal Court," p. 867.

CHAPTER 6

STRANDED BETWEEN TWO RECEDING SHORELINES? THE ANGLO-AMERICAN SPECIAL RELATIONSHIP AFTER THE MAY 5, 2005, ELECTIONS

Mark Gilbert

In the days immediately before Britain's general election on May 5, 2005, one revealing insight into the politics of the "special relationship" between Britain and the United States was provided by typing the phrases "Tony Blair Special Relationship" and "Michael Howard Special Relationship" into Google. In the former case, the inquirer obtained thousands of hits and was able to access dozens of articles and think-tank commentaries on the importance of the Anglo-American partnership for world affairs. In the second case, the inquirer was presented mostly with a long list of speeches by Conservative leader Howard on the sanctity of marriage.

This anecdote reveals the difficulty Michael Howard has encountered in formulating a policy toward the United States that differs in any significant way from the prime minister's. Mr. Blair has been one of a handful of British leaders who have influenced American policy successfully and, as a result, heightened British standing in Washington and the world in general. Ernest Bevin pulled this trick off; so, more unctuously, did Harold Macmillan. Anthony Eden disastrously failed; Harold Wilson exasperated Lyndon B. Johnson by jetting into Washington for an impromptu summit every time his poll ratings were slipping; Edward Heath, though he maintained a formal veneer of good relations with the Nixon White House, distrusted and disliked U.S. policy and did his best to encourage the emergence of a common European Community foreign policy in opposition to that of the United States.

In part, the success or failure of the special relationship reflects personal chemistry between leaders. Bevin was esteemed and perhaps even slightly feared by his American counterparts. Macmillan and Kennedy, despite the age difference, do seem to have developed a mutual personal respect, as did George Bush senior and John Major.

Thatcher and Reagan, at any rate in public, were a mutual admiration society. George W. Bush and Tony Blair, with their shared concern for religious values and worries about moral decadence, seem to have established an authentic friendship that seemed improbable in light of Mr. Blair's even closer friendship with President Clinton.[1]

But it seems clear that circumstances are more important than personal chemistry. The British statesmen who enjoyed the most influence in Washington were those in power at moments when the United States needed military, moral, or political support. Berlin could not have been saved during the early Cold War, the North Atlantic Treaty could not have been negotiated, and South Korea could not have been preserved without the giant figure of Ernest Bevin and the less great, but underestimated figure of Clement Attlee. Thatcher's hostility to communism and her outspoken championing of free-market values were extremely useful to the United States in the early years of the Reagan presidency. Tony Blair, meanwhile, has given a gloss of respectability to the U.S.-led Iraq war and made it appear less of an exercise in high-tech gunboat diplomacy.

Not surprisingly, the special relationship has been at its worst when Britain was perceived in Washington to have let the Americans down. Eden, whether from imperial hubris, lack of comprehension of the American position, or sheer irritability, hopelessly antagonized the United States, which was determined not to take sides in a conflict between colonialism and third world nationalism, by his policy towards Egypt in October-November 1956.[2] Wilson could have gotten away with reducing British commitments "East of Suez," or with failing to commit troops in Vietnam, or with devaluing the pound; but his failure to live up to expectations on all three counts lost him Lyndon Johnson's goodwill.[3]

A warm special relationship therefore depends upon: (1) the U.S. need for British support for its immediate foreign policy goals, and (2) British policy being coherent with broader American objectives. This may sound banal, but I think the point is worth emphasizing, since the special relationship is suffused with so much sub-Churchillian rhetoric about cultural unities and our great common history. While it is no doubt true, to quote John Major, that "there is a unique rapport between Britain and the United States," the undoubted cultural closeness of Britain and the United States has not guaranteed idyllic relations in the past, and does not guarantee that the two countries will remain on good terms in the near future. The two countries' interests, as Major himself admitted, can diverge.[4]

It is also worth remembering that the cultural similarities between the two nations can easily be taken for granted. Nations change over time. Although the United States unquestionably continues to be a very attractive society for many British citizens, and large parts of the British establishment certainly retain a deep respect for U.S. institutions, generosity, and military know-how, it is also true that this admiration is in many ways a remembrance of things passing. U.S. soft power reserves will be exhausted eventually, even in Britain, if she continues her present trend towards vociferous moral conservatism and unabashed hyper-patriotism. A society as deeply secular as Britain (weekly church attendance is well under 10 percent of the adult population, and the number of professing Christians is, by American standards, derisory) is not a natural partner for an American polity throbbing with moral majority rhetoric and action. On Sundays, most Britons wash their cars, trudge glumly around shopping malls, or worship do-it-yourself sofas at IKEA.

Will the United States Need Britain?

So the first question is: Will the United States continue to need British support? The obvious answer is "yes." Any regular reader of the quality press, or even *The Times*, could quickly reel off a list of reasons: (a) The United States needs British support in Iraq to help maintain order and to ease the transition to democracy; (b) The United States needs Britain to act, in Tony Blair's somewhat clichéd metaphor, as a "bridge" between the two banks of the Atlantic; (c) the two countries cooperate over intelligence matters; (d) Britain is a useful veto-wielding ally in the United Nations Security Council (UNSC). In short, Britain is needed by the United States in order to make superpowerdom a little less lonely.

These are all good reasons for thinking that the United States will continue to need Britain. Whether she will continue to need Britain quite so intensely is another matter. This surely depends largely upon events. If North Korea implodes, Japan, South Korea, and China will become the focus of American diplomacy; and Junichiro Koizumi, or his successor, will eclipse Tony Blair in importance. The same is true if a crisis should blow up between China and Taiwan. If tensions grow between Ukraine and Russia, Germany and Poland would weigh at least as heavily on American scales as Britain, and probably more. One can multiply the examples. The point is that since September 11, 2001, circumstances have conspired to place Britain at the heart of U.S. concerns (and Britain's leaders certainly have exploited the situation with skill). But this need not be a permanent state of affairs.

Will British Policy Remain Coherent with that of the United States?

This is the more interesting and problematic question. Several factors might easily affect British policy toward the United States, the recent British general election for one. As expected, the Labour Party won a third successive electoral victory on May 5, 2005, but its majority was slashed by almost 100 seats. Mr. Blair can now count on a majority of just 67 seats in the House of Commons. For most third-term governments, a victory of this kind would be regarded as a considerable success. But as most commentators immediately recognized, in Blair's case a majority of these dimensions has to be considered a personal defeat for the Prime Minister.

The reason is that, in terms of votes, Labour's performance was decidedly unimpressive. Labour lost votes to the Conservatives and barely came out ahead of them in the popular vote (35 vs. 32 percent). Overall, New Labour won just 9.6 million votes—hardly more than a fifth of Britain's adult population. The two main Opposition parties—the Conservatives and the Liberal Democrats—together took 15 million votes. It is fair to say that the lopsidedness of the British "winner-takes-all" electoral system rarely has been so vividly demonstrated.

Moreover, Labour's unimpressive results were achieved against dismal opposition. The Conservative Party's populist positions on a number of sensitive questions such as Europe, immigration, and crime, while appealing to a hard core of working class supporters, unnerved middle class centrists and obstructed the party's return to the center ground in which British elections are won or lost. Michael Howard rightly fell on his sword when the mediocre nature of the Conservative Party's electoral improvement became clear. Liberal Democrat leader Charles Kennedy could boast a gain of 11 new Ministers of Parliament (MPs) as compared to 2001 and a total of almost six million votes (22 percent), but Mr. Kennedy failed to impress as a leader during the electoral campaign and must now be regretting that he did not invade the political center more vigorously. The Liberal Democrats picked up many voters from Labour's left, but did not modernize their traditional tax and spend policies to attract moderate Conservatives. It is hard to escape the conclusion that a centrist Tory with charisma — admittedly a rare beast — could and would have put Mr. Blair's majority at risk. But the truth of the witticism that Mr. Blair remains the only centrist Tory politician in Britain was confirmed by the election campaign.

What will be the likely consequences of Mr. Blair's muted victory for the relationship with the United States? Mr. Blair is the most pro-American Labour leader imaginable, and after a "defeat" of this kind he may not hold the office of prime minister for a full 5 years. His likely successor, Chancellor of the Exchequer Gordon Brown, is certainly an admirer of many aspects of the American economy and political system, but he is also more closely associated with the Labour grassroots than Mr. Blair. Many ordinary Labour members have been angered by the closeness of Blair's ties with President Bush. A third of the Labour Party's parliamentary contingent voted against the campaign in Iraq. Anybody who wants to know what ordinary Labour supporters (and many backbenchers) think about the United States need only read the *Guardian* or the *New Statesman*. These two newspapers at times have been hysterically anti-American since September 11, with the *tone* of their criticism going far beyond what even a highly negative evaluation of U.S. foreign policy might justify.[5] After the May election, if only because the Blairite MPs from southern England have borne the brunt of the electoral losses, the likelihood is that the mood of the Labour Party will be less amenable to unconditional support for U.S. foreign policy. Mr. Brown probably will not put his leadership chances in jeopardy by publicly contradicting this mood. He has waited too long to be leader.

Much of the public disaffection with Blair is linked to the continuing Iraq crisis and the widespread perception that the Prime Minister had misled parliament and the public about Iraq's weapons of mass destruction during the run-up to the second Gulf War. These issues were also a decisive factor in Labour's poor performance in the recent election. The most striking individual victory in the election was secured by "Gorgeous George" Galloway, a pro-Iraqi ex-Labour MP, who formed the anti-war "Respect" party and campaigned in the London constituency of Bethnal Green and Bow, which has a large Muslim population. Mr. Galloway, who has been implicated in the United Nations (UN) "oil for food" scandal, but who strongly denies any wrongdoing, won a shattering victory against the Labour candidate. In his victory speech, he dedicated his votes to the people of Iraq and warned Mr. Blair that "all the people you have killed and all the loss of life have come back to haunt you, and the best thing the Labour party can do is sack you tomorrow morning." Reg Keys, the father of a military policeman killed in Iraq, campaigned personally against Mr. Blair in his County Durham constituency and obtained 4,252 votes—hardly a negligible figure for an individual citizen without party support and organization.

Indeed, there are already strong signs that the Labour Party's left is drawing lines in the sand that Mr. Blair will cross at his peril. Shortly before the election, former Foreign Secretary and Iraq war rebel Robin Cook contributed a significant article to the *Guardian* entitled "Why American Neocons Are Out for Kofi Annan's Blood." Cook's theme in this article was that the U.S. right is leading the attack on the UN Secretary General precisely because Mr. Annan is a reformer who wishes to see improved global governance. More generally, Cook asserted:

> The world is confronted with a choice between two competing models of global governance. The direction signposted by Kofi Annan is to a regenerated UN with new authority for its collective decisions. However, collective decisionmaking is only possible if there is broad equivalence among those taking part. And there is the rub. The neocons who run the U.S. administration want supremacy, not equality, for America and hanker after an alternative model of global governance in which the

world is put to right not by the tedious process of building international consensus, but by the straightforward exercise of U.S. puissance.[6]

The woolly-mindedness of this passage doubtless will raise hackles in some U.S. circles. There is not "broad equivalence" among the major nation-states of the world today—some nations are plainly more equal than others. Robin Cook is, in substance, asking the United States to pretend it is Canada for the sake of international "governance"—whatever this buzzword actually means. Presumably, this will not happen. But it is certainly true that Mr. Cook speaks for many, perhaps most, Labour backbenchers when he expresses such views, and that these backbenchers, many of whom feel betrayed by Mr. Blair's foreign policy since 2001, will vote, if necessary, against the government. It is clear that British support for further U.S. intervention anywhere in the world will be conditional upon there having been blatant breaches of international law. As Gerald Dorfman perceptively has argued, "Britain will be more hesitant and sceptical about embracing American initiatives and about committing its military to war."[7] Iraq has exhausted British enthusiasm for military conflicts undertaken at U.S. behest and on the basis of chancy photographs.

Mr. Blair's foreign policy priorities in any case may not be as accommodating to the United States as most people think. As Blair powerfully argued at the Davos World Economic summit on January 26, 2005, Britain's priorities during the meeting of G-8 (consisting of France, the United States, Britain, Germany, Japan, Italy, Canada, and Russia) and European Union (EU) presidencies would be global warming and world poverty.[8] Perhaps sensing that Blair would trim his coat to suit his cloth, the *Guardian* urged Blair to give salience in his foreign policy to issues such as poverty and development, AIDS, and Third World debt, and to "use his clout to ensure Washington sticks firmly to the road map to Israeli-Palestinian peace."[9] While such objectives are not necessarily contrary to U.S. priorities—as the Gleneagles accord in early July 2005 showed—they do suggest that Blair is not concentrating single-mindedly either on the war on terror or on the special relationship. Blair's leadership on this score already has paid dividends in Europe, where British adherence to the Nordic countries' long-term pressure for a greater aid commitment has led to the EU states making, on May 24, 2005, a powerful pledge to spend a substantially increased portion of gross domestic product (GDP) on aid to the Third World and Africa in particular. In Europe, this commitment was interpreted widely as an alternative foreign policy to that preferred by George W. Bush.

In the same Davos speech, Blair went out of his way to stress that "interdependence is the governing characteristic of modern international politics" and that "international engagement" of the major power groups was essential. Blair's political antenna is probably the most sophisticated of any contemporary political leader. He is well aware that U.S. unilateralism has outlived its welcome with British public opinion. Concentrating his efforts on building coalitions willing to deal with some major international problems is a strategy that has obvious appeal for a man, like Mr. Blair, who sincerely loves to do good, but who also likes to do well. The strategy has obvious personal benefits for the British Prime Minister. The kudos he receives from the left in both Europe and the United States will compensate for any chilliness that might ensue in his relations with Washington.

Another factor that might cause the new Labour government to cool towards the Atlantic relationship is the strength of its ties with the EU. Given the high profile of the Labour government's Atlantic policy, it is easy to forget that Blair and Foreign Secretary Jack Straw have followed a very active European policy. Despite the Iraq diversion, Blair has largely continued, with no little success, John Major's policy of placing Britain at the "heart of Europe." Essentially, this campaign involves combating the federalist aspirations evoked in Europe in the 1990s by Jacques Delors and, later, Joschka Fischer, while presenting an alternative vision of an enlarged economic confederation of 20-plus states that respects the central decisionmaking role and political rights of the member states.

Who can dispute the success of British diplomacy in this regard? Contrary to the beliefs of the flakier British Conservatives and Euroskeptics, the current EU — with its various national opt-outs, its (still incomplete) single market, its (failing) competitiveness agenda, its strictly limited budgetary resources (Britain, the Netherlands, and Germany want to restrict the budget to 1 percent of Gross Union

Product; it currently may not be more than 1.27 percent), and its sturdily intergovernmental approach to decisionmaking on major questions—is to a significant extent a *British* creation. Anybody who has studied the history of European integration since the 1986 Single European Act will know this.

Moreover, Britain played an active role in promoting EU enlargement to embrace the new democracies of Central and Eastern Europe and played a decisive part in ensuring that relatively few concessions were made to supranationalist principles in the EU Constitution that was signed in Rome at the end of October 2004—an outcome that was far from certain when the constitutional process began in March 2001. The final version of the Constitution has Britain's sticky fingerprints all over it. All the main policy areas will continue to be decided by unanimity; the role of the European Council is strengthened; matters decided by qualified majority voting will pass only with a very high degree of consensus, despite the influx of new members; the Union's competences have been rigidly fixed; national parliaments will possess a de facto veto over controversial legislation; and amending the Constitution will be extremely difficult.[10] It is not an accident that one of the main reasons given by French opponents of the Constitution during the electoral campaign prior to France's dramatic rejection of the new Constitution on May 27, 2005, was that the document is much too "Anglo-Saxon" in character.

With success comes responsibility. Britain would lose all credibility within the EU, and its diplomatic achievement would accordingly be threatened, were she to take America's side consistently in all the disputes currently upsetting relations between the EU and the United States. London, and Mr. Blair personally, cannot allow critics across the Channel to cast doubt on Britain's European credentials by depicting the Prime Minister as America's poodle.

But, unfortunately, there are plenty of grounds for U.S.-EU disagreement. Despite President Bush's recent charm offensive, which included his heartfelt appeal for a "new era of transatlantic unity" in a speech in Brussels in February 2005, arms to China, vital trade questions such as the Boeing/Airbus row, the ongoing conflict in Iraq, and the Iran nuclear question all divide the United States from most of the important EU states. If Britain *is* a "bridge" over the Atlantic, she risks finding herself stranded between two rapidly receding shorelines. If she is constrained to *build* bridges towards one bank or the other, it is possible that she may not choose the traditional route towards the United States.

The question is complicated by the fact that the EU is likely to prove a tricky diplomatic arena during the lifetime of the current Labour government. The next 5 years seem likely to be the most problematic period in European integration since the near-breakdown of the European Community in the early 1980s. The French and Dutch referendums in May-June 2005 have thrown the EU into total confusion; there is bound to be a concerted attempt to make Britain surrender its supposedly permanent rebate on its contribution to the EU budget. Furthermore, protectionist sentiment may grow in the EU, leaving neo-liberal Britain with no choice but to fight a series of hard battles from within the EU.

This turbulent situation is both a threat and an opportunity for Britain. Mr. Blair may use the crisis in the EU to wrench leadership of the Union from the hands of France and Germany and shift the EU towards the liberalization agenda he clearly prefers. On the other hand, it is quite possible that Britain will be made a scapegoat for the Union's present travails. In the latter case, the special relationship with the United States may come to seem a safe haven from the growing chaos of European entanglements. Macmillan's famous admonition that we should never forget "events, dear boy, events" still holds good.

American Perspectives.

From an American perspective, therefore, the state of the special relationship is bound to be a delicate one over the next few years. British political and public opinion will warm only to a more multilateralist United States that eschews the "robust brand of internationalism" practiced in recent years.[11] Britain will also have a Prime Minister who will raise issues that Americans may want to sweep under the carpet. Britain will also certainly be embroiled — this is the right word — in the internal politics of an EU whose purpose is increasingly contested and whose chief policy orientations are under threat.

From the American perspective, therefore, the central future political question of the special relationship, assuming the United

States continues to regard the Atlantic link as a cornerstone of its policy, lies in understanding that Britain is less different than she often seems from the rest of the big EU states. Britain, while far more pro-American than almost any other European country, nevertheless shares some of Europe's disquiet at current U.S. foreign policy and is alarmed by many of the same global trends as her European neighbors. Moreover, the paradox of Britain's strongly "euro-sceptical" public mood is that the United Kingdom (UK) is arguably the most Brussels-obsessed country in the whole of the EU (British public and political opinion rightly dedicate enormous attention to what is happening in Brussels).

Britain is also not Berlusconi's Italy. She won't necessarily jump if the United States barks. Consider, for example, the following assertion (which I note from a 2002 article by a neoconservative author but which reflects a still-relevant strain of U.S. policy thinking): "[I]f Washington insists on Britain reshaping (or scuppering) European military plans, desisting from further European integration, and renewing its transatlantic focus, London will comply." This assertion greatly misunderstands the complexity of the special relationship today.[12] Nowadays an old-fashioned "command and obey" approach to marriage often leads to one spouse slamming the door on her way to her lawyer. The special relationship, like any other relationship, could fray at the edges if the United States becomes domineering and insists that Britain drop her friends.

If this statement is true, and if the considerations I outlined earlier about the U.S. *need* for the special relationship are also true, the U.S. task thereupon becomes that of *helping* the UK to remain in the U.S. camp. How can this be done? Continuing to accord Tony Blair a special status among international leaders will do no harm. Making the right noises (and writing some of the right checks) on global poverty, global warming, and the Palestinian question will positively do good. Avoiding unilateral strikes against rogue states is essential. Publicly acknowledging that the U.S. society contains blemishes and imperfections and that recent U.S. foreign policy has not been a triumphal chapter in the struggle to promote democracy would do most good of all, but expecting self-criticism from a hegemon is probably a forlorn hope. After all, the British political élite were prone to the same kinds of rhetorical excess before the sun set on the British empire.

U.S. policy towards Europe also will influence the future of the special relationship. There appears to be a growing perception in Washington policy circles—a perception encouraged by many prominent EU boosters—that the EU is a major threat to American hegemony in the West.[13] Some voices therefore have been urging that the EU should be humbled before it challenges the U.S. leadership role. Suggestions for dissolving the EU's power range from the crude to the sophisticated. An example of the latter has been advanced by John C. Hulsman, in a series of very well-researched and stimulating Heritage Foundation lectures and position papers (and in his chapter in this book).[14] Hulsman contends that the United States should "cherry-pick" the more Atlanticist member states of the EU, with Britain obviously being the chief prize, to form a Global Free Trade Association (GFTA) parallel to the EU.

This idea, which, if put into practice, would undermine one of the EU's most solid historical achievements—its ability to act as a bloc in trade talks—has obvious similarities with Britain's 1957 proposal for a European Free Trade Association (EFTA) and suffers from exactly the same defects. Like EFTA, it gives its main proponent (the United States) far too many economic benefits in exchange for far too little loss in sovereignty. After the experience of European integration, where free trade measures within the Community have been locked in by a series of treaties that have direct legal effect upon the citizens of the member states, few EU members, Britain included, would be enthused about joining an organization whose trade bargains would depend entirely upon the whim of the majority in Congress for their durability. The great advantage of the EU is that free trade within the Community is backed by law. Moreover, just as EFTA was seen as an attempt to dissolve the European Economic Community (EEC) like a "lump of sugar in a cup of hot tea," so GFTA would inevitably be interpreted as a scheme to dismantle the EU. A possible result of this, especially in the light of the anti-globalization rhetoric so dominant during the French referendum, might be the formation of an anti-American and protection-inclined bloc of states within the EU. This would be in neither U.S. nor British interests.

The GFTA plan may be a useful "Plan B" for the United States if the EU plunges back into the futile bickering over budgets and institutions that characterized the EC in the early 1980s. John

Hulsman is right to stress that there is a widening cleavage between the EU's dinosaurs (France is an obvious example, but Italy is an even more striking case) and its more liberal-minded members (the flat-taxers of Central Europe and the Baltic, Ireland, Britain, but also modernized and competitive social democratic states like Denmark, Finland, and the Netherlands). Contrary to the mythology of the European movement, which has always assumed that progress to full political union was inevitable in the long march of history, this cleavage might easily have substantial political consequences in the next 5 to 10 years, and defections cannot be ruled out.

A better U.S. response, however, surely would be to intensify the "charm offensive" launched by President Bush and Secretary of State Condoleeza Rice, by encouraging more high-level political dialogue between the United States and the European nations. Jaw jaw is better than war war. There are already multiple forums for transatlantic cooperation, notably the Euro-Atlantic Partnership Council and the G-8, and it may be that further such institutions need to be developed. Why should there not, for instance, be a formal and regular Atlantic Economic Council, attended not only by government officials but by Congressmen and members of the European and national Parliaments which would be empowered to hold hearings, debate, and make recommendations to the national governments about trade questions, currency issues, and other pertinent matters? No sovereignty would be lost on either side, but both the U.S. trade administrator and the European Commissioner for trade would be forced to justify their positions in open debate. Progress might possibly accelerate as a result. At any rate, an understanding of why progress must be slow or nonexistent might be more widely diffused, and the relationship between the EU and the United States might seem less confrontational.

Future political developments within Western Europe might make such transatlantic engagement a more promising strategy than it may currently appear. A Christian Democrat Germany, led by Angela Merkel, surely will prove to be more Atlanticist than the SPD-Green administration. At a minimum, a Merkel-led Germany will be unlikely deliberately to whip up anti-Americanism for electoral purposes. A post-Berlusconi Italy, governed by the center-left, while it will be less instinctively pro-American than the current government has been, will inevitably be open to persuasion and will not want to appear anti-American. France and Spain, if the United States could swallow its understandable annoyance with Jacques Chirac and José Luis Zapatero, might prove surprisingly responsive. Most important of all, Britain would welcome a re-launched Atlanticism as an opportunity to exercise leadership within Europe and to fulfil her bridging role.

What this chapter has sought to underline, in short, is that in its European policy, the United States must not put Britain in the position where she has no choice but to break with Europe or break with the United States. Such a policy would be stupid diplomatically and might not have the intended results.

It is worth remarking in conclusion that the current conjuncture offers enormous opportunities for statesmanship. As a very thoughtful book by MIT political scientist Richard Samuels recently has argued, the ability of leaders to "stretch constraints" is the definition of statesmanship. Leaders of stature are those who see opportunities for constructive initiatives when less gifted politicians see themselves as being hemmed in by the circumstances of their time.[15] The current state of transatlantic relations is one such opportunity. As John Lewis Gaddis has argued, Washington needs to re-learn the art of "speaking more softly" and to remember that "it is never a good idea to insult potential allies, however outrageous their behaviour may have been."[16] If the United States can engage with Europe, institutionally and intellectually, she will lose little and may gain much. Certainly she will strengthen the relationship with Britain, which, as I have been suggesting, is shakier than many Americans think. Antagonism between the United States and Europe will leave Britain, to repeat the metaphor used once already in this chapter, "stranded between receding shorelines." Such a situation would be a crisis for Britain, but it would be a grave problem for the United States as well.

ENDNOTES - CHAPTER 6

1. For Blair's friendship with Clinton and Bush, see P. Stephens, *Tony Blair: The Making of a World Leader*, New York, Viking, 2004, especially chaps 4, 7, and 11.

2. On Suez, the literature is vast. D. R. Thorpe, *Eden: The Life and Times of Anthony Eden*, London: Pimlico, 2003, gives a compressed and more sympathetic account than usual of Eden's behavior during the crisis.

3. For Wilson and Johnson, I recommend J. Colman, *A 'Special Relationship'? Harold Wilson, Lyndon B. Johnson and Anglo-American Relations 'at the Summit', 1964-68*, Manchester, England: Manchester University Press, 2004.

4. John Major, *John Major: The Autobiography*, London: HarperCollins, 2000, p. 496.

5. See Mark Gilbert, "Superman versus Lex Luther: British Anti-Americanism since September 11," *World Policy Journal*, Vol. 19, No. 2, Summer 2002, pp. 88-92.

6. Robin Cook, "Why American Neocons Are Out for Kofi Annan's Blood," *Guardian*, April 1, 2005.

7. Gerald Dorfman, "Trouble at Number Ten," *Hoover Digest* 2005, n. 1.

8. Tony Blair, speech to the World Economic Forum, Davos, Switzerland, January 26, 2005, *http://www.number-10.gov.uk*.

9. *Guardian*, Leading article, May 13, 2005.

10. See Foreign and Commonwealth Office, *White Paper on Treaty Establishing a Constitution for Europe*, Command 6309, September 2004, for Britain's satisfaction with the Constitution.

11. The phrase by Robert Kagan and William Kristol in their introduction to *Present Dangers: Crisis and Opportunity in American Defense Policy*, San Francisco, CA: Encounter Books, 2000, p. 23.

12. Robin Harris, "The State of the Special Relationship," *Policy Review*, No. 113, June 2002, p. 7 of online version.

13. For American fears, see Jeffrey L. Cimbalo, "Saving NATO from Europe, *Foreign Affairs*, November/December 2004; Mark Leonard, *Why Europe Will Run the 21st Century*, London, Fourth Estate, 2005; and, egregiously, Stephen Haseler, *Super-state: The New Europe and Its Challenge to America*, New York: I. B. Taurus, 2004.

14. See, especially, John C. Hulsman, "European Arrogance and Weakness Dictate Coalitions of the Willing," Heritage Lecture No. 777, December 19, 2002; and, with Nile Gardiner, "President Bush Should Advance a New U.S. Vision for Europe," Heritage Foundation Backgrounder No. 1825, February 18, 2005, which actually comes quite close in its analysis to the position I've been taking here.

15. Richard J. Samuels, *Machiavelli's Children: Leaders and their Legacies in Italy and Japan*, Ithaca, NY: Cornell University Press, 2003, p. 7.

16. John Lewis Gaddis, "Grand Strategy in the Second Term," *Foreign Affairs*, January/February 2005. Quotations are from pp. 2, 3 of the online edition.

CHAPTER 7

POLITICAL AND LEGAL ASPECTS OF THE SPECIAL
RELATIONSHIP: PANEL CHAIRMAN'S SUMMARY
AND RECOMMENDATIONS

Andrew Apostolou

The German statesman Bismarck reportedly once prophesied that the most important fact of the oncoming 20th century would be that Britain and America spoke the same language. Subsequent German leaders would discover that Bismarck was accurate in his prediction as to the weighty consequences of the bond between the two countries. Yet, at the time of the attributed comment, the late 19th century, British-American relations were socially friendly but politically somewhat cooler. Lord Randolph Churchill, Maurice Crawford MacMillan, and Joseph Chamberlain married American heiresses, and offspring from the first two unions became British prime ministers. However, in 1890, the same year that the American Naval officer, Captain Alfred Thayer Mahan, published *The Influence of Sea Power Upon History, 1660-1783*, he also drew up a "Contingency Plan of Operations in Case of War with Great Britain."[1] In 1902, British prime minister Lord Salisbury wrote concerning growing U.S. naval strength: "It is very sad, but I am afraid America is bound to forge ahead and nothing can restore the equality between us."[2]

So much, then, for the mawkish nostalgia and high-flown rhetoric about our common history that tends to bubble to the surface when the "special relationship" is discussed. With useful sobriety and illuminating detail, Professor Douglas Edlin of Dickinson College and Professor Mark Gilbert of the University of Trento in Italy remind us in their chapters on the legal and political aspects of the special relationship of the practicalities of the British-American alliance. Beneath the grandiose speeches celebrating that relationship, and the recent shrill denunciations of it, there are hard legal and political questions that we must confront. Edlin and Gilbert have done just that.

Edlin on the ICC.

One of the most troubling issues in recent years has been divergent transatlantic attitudes regarding international law. Not only have there been questions raised about the legality, or otherwise, of the Iraq war, but U.S. tactics in the war against terrorism also have come under scrutiny. In Chapter 5, Edlin provides a detailed analysis of an issue that predated both of these controversies, but that also overshadows them: the U.S. government's decision not to join the International Criminal Court (ICC). The purpose of the ICC is to prosecute four types of major war crime—genocide, crimes against humanity, crimes in war, and aggression—if national courts are unwilling or unable to do so. So hostile is the United States to the ICC that it has adopted legislation that protects its officials and servicemen from potential ICC jurisdiction, no matter how unlikely that is. By contrast, Great Britain has both signed and ratified the Rome Statute (the ICC's charter) and was an important player in crafting it.

Edlin's accessible and carefully structured analysis avoids the obvious positions—the first being the "everybody-does-it" defense, suggesting that all nations adapt international law to their convenience; and the second being the anti-U.S. reflex of invoking an imagined international legal system as a justification for attempting to tie the United States in juridical knots. Instead, Edlin outlines the four key aspects of the ICC that the United States finds objectionable and considers whether these arguments are well-founded. Not surprisingly, many U.S. objections ultimately stem from concerns over sovereignty.

First, the ICC is criticized for unfair procedures that are at odds with the American constitution and that allow the ICC, an unaccountable body, to sit in judgment over the United States. Edlin observes that some of these claims do not stand up to scrutiny, and that ICC procedures do not differ much from the congressionally-enacted Universal Code of Military Justice applicable to the U.S. armed forces. War crimes prosecutions and domestic criminal prosecutions are very different and, indeed, are supposed to be.

Second, the ICC is accused of attempting to bind nonparties, which is objectionable under the usual international legal practice that treaties apply only to those who have signed and ratified them. However, in the past the United States has acceded to treaties that have similar reach.

Third, some critics worry that the ICC may engage in frivolous, politicized prosecutions of Americans. In fact, the ICC can take a case only if national courts either will not or cannot do so. However, the ICC can, in essence, earmark a case for future prosecution if it suspects that national proceedings are a means of protecting persons from legal jeopardy.

Fourth, the ICC is opposed on the grounds that it is unaccountable. The United States wanted the ICC to be required to seek permission from the United Nations (UN) Security Council to proceed with a case. Great Britain, which initially took a similar stance, was willing to forgo this requirement. Making the ICC independent of the UN Security Council is, in fact, problematic — witness the way the UN General Assembly sidelined the Council by referring the Israeli security barrier case to the International Court of Justice (ICJ). At the same time, however, separating the ICC from the Council gives the Court an aura of independence. Indeed, the British-American legal tradition is the key champion of this principle of judicial independence.

American opposition to the ICC has potentially great ramifications. The U.S. commitment to the rule of law appears, Edlin argues, to have been weakened by the American stance on the ICC, a stance that limits U.S. influence. There are, in addition, implications for future military operations. British and American forces fight and operate side-by-side in a number of different theaters, which makes mutually-agreed legal standards and rules of engagement critical. For example, British forces apply the Geneva Conventions in their counterterrorism operations in Afghanistan, while U.S. forces do not.

During the discussion of Professor Edlin's paper, it became clear that no U.S. administration was likely to have gained congressional support for the ICC. This generated various questions. Could the U.S. government have dealt with the ICC issue more shrewdly? Could the United States have dodged both ratifying the ICC statute and the resulting opprobrium? As one participant asked, was there not a better alternative to just saying "no"? Could the United States have responded more constructively? The merits or demerits of the ICC notwithstanding, the diplomacy involved has not been impressive. President William Clinton's administration signed the Rome Statute on the very last day of the signing period, December 31, 2000. President Clinton thereby acceded to a treaty that he knew the incoming Bush administration opposed and that, even had the presidential election result in 2000 been different, stood little chance of being ratified by the U.S. Senate. President George W. Bush then "unsigned" the Rome Statute on May 6, 2002. Both decisions made little political sense. For his part, President Bush renounced the treaty and ignited controversy, making the United States an easy target for criticism, when all he had to do was to allow the Rome statute to be shelved, or rejected, by the Senate.

The disagreement over the ICC has also had practical consequences, such as for the people of Darfur in western Sudan. Both sides of the argument have been able to manipulate the ICC controversy in a way enabling them to evade acting in the Darfur crisis. Neither the United States nor the critics of the its attitude toward international law in the European Union (EU) have any desire to take concrete measures to end the mass killings in Darfur. The United States correctly has declared Darfur to be genocide, even while it cooperates against terrorism with a Sudanese government that is largely responsible for that genocide and that was previously responsible for the terrorism. Invoking the word "genocide" but not taking action, or demanding that the UN act, is posturing. Many in the EU (Sweden is an exception)[3] shrink from calling the mass killings in Darfur genocide because such a finding by the UN would oblige international action, action that would either threaten their national interests or expose their lack of capabilities. Instead, they are content with the findings of a UN panel that carefully danced around this issue and that recommended referring the atrocities in Darfur to the ICC.[4] That way, they also strike an attitude which implies that they care about the Darfur crisis, while reminding the world that they back the ICC and the United States does not.

Fundamentally, however, there is also a clash of legal traditions at work here. Thomas Buergenthal, an American justice on the ICJ, has described this difference compellingly:

For much of our history, we have been able to look for protection to American courts and political institutions rather than to international human rights law and institutions when our human rights appeared to be threatened. This explains, I believe, why we tend not to appreciate why people in other countries often attach such great importance to international judicial and quasi-judicial human rights institutions and to human rights treaties.[5]

Gilbert on British Politics and the Special Relationship.

Professor Mark Gilbert's Chapter 6, prepared before the British general election and the EU crisis that followed the French and Dutch rejections of the new EU constitution, has held up extremely well to these changing events—requiring only small editorial updates for his contribution to this volume. Gilbert brushed aside what he called the "sub-Churchillian rhetoric about cultural unities and our great common history," and instead analyzed the circumstances under which the special relationship had flourished. With a keen judgment of personalities, he described how personal relations between the president of the United States and the prime minister of Great Britain have played a role in bilateral relations. But three other factors, he argued, were even more critical: first, that the United States needs Great Britain to support its foreign policy; second, that British policy is coherently consistent with that of the United States; and, third, that the UK must not be perceived by Washington as letting the United States down. The special relationship is at its worst when this third condition is not fulfilled. Gilbert nonetheless concluded by arguing that leadership does matter, and that good leaders stretch constraints, refusing to allow themselves to be locked in by them.

In Gilbert's judgment, Tony Blair has been weakened by the result of the British elections. However, context matters. The terrorist attacks in London on July 7, 2005, and Blair's strong leadership in their aftermath, have caused some to wonder whether he will, as he has promised, step down by the time of the next general election.[6] It is hard to imagine any other British politician having the necessary skills and vision to rally the country in time of crisis and war. Furthermore, the EU crisis that began with the French rejection of the EU constitution in May 2005 has delivered a severe blow to the notion of the EU either as a rival pole of attraction for Britain's primary loyalties or as a rival power to the United States in global affairs. Fears of the EU as a potential rival to the United States generally are exaggerated in any event. It is interesting to note that the U.S. government, in a policy review in early 2005, chose to retain its long-standing support of EU integration because, as the State Department successfully argued (in the face of Department of Defense [DoD] skepticism), the anti-Americanism represented by Jacques Chirac and Gerhard Schroeder would end when they left office, and their likely successors would probably take a more pro-U.S. stance. As one conference participant wisely observed, while the United States rates poorly in opinion polls in the EU, so does the EU itself.

Gilbert called the current crisis in the EU "a threat and an opportunity for Britain." The silly posturing over "freedom fries" (vice French fries) has masked the deep sense of disappointment in Chirac felt by the UK government.[7] Blair was willing to accept some stress to the close defense ties between the United States and Great Britain by agreeing to Chirac's demands at St. Malo, France, in 1998 that the EU enhance its defense and security identity. The subsequent belief in London that Chirac ambushed the United States and Britain at the UN over Iraq and actively sought to engineer Tony Blair's political downfall engendered antipathy that extends well beyond the culinary. While Blair publicly bemoaned the French and Dutch rejection of the EU constitution (a document that Gilbert astutely argues had represented a victory for British diplomacy), few doubt Blair's satisfaction in seeing Chirac take the bullet for him.

In the light of recent EU developments, Blair looks downright strong, especially when the damage inflicted by the French and Dutch rejection of the EU constitution on both Chirac and Schroeder is given due weight.[8] Indeed, commentators who have been busily interring the special relationship and its most eloquent advocate, the British prime minister, have now found that he is the last man standing in EU politics.

The British-American special relationship does face some serious problems, however, especially with some sections of British public opinion. Three explanations bear particular mention. First, the inequality in the relationship is bound to rankle from time to time in Britain. That the special relationship has endured as long as it has and survived repeated predictions of imminent demise is remarkable. The world is not replete with examples of former great powers that accept a demotion to junior partner status as the price of salvation. The British are the reliable allies of the Americans. There is great admiration throughout the United States for Great Britain's staunch loyalty and contribution to the war against Islamist terrorism and in Iraq, in obvious contrast to the behavior of other EU states. In fact, one of the few items of agreement between George W. Bush and John Kerry during the presidential election foreign policy debate on September 30, 2004, was their respect for Tony Blair.[9] On the other hand, Blair's image in the United States as a reliable ally and a "stand-up kind of guy" who demonstrates "backbone and courage and strong leadership" (President George W. Bush's words),[10] has been the source of much of the bilious criticism by the British press that the Prime Minister is "Bush's poodle."[11]

There has been a shift in British public opinion against the United States, but it is not as dramatic as the British news media would have us believe. According to the most recent poll from the Pew Research Center, 55 percent of British respondents have a favorable view of the United States (admittedly, a sharp drop from 83 percent in 1999/2000).[12] Interestingly, those with low incomes view the United States more favorably than those with high incomes (57.6 percent of low income Britons say that the United States is mostly a positive factor in the world, compared to 37.1 percent of those with high incomes).[13] The British news media's exaggeration of anti-Americanism thus stems from the simple fact that those who work in newspapers and television generally are not from Britain's poorest classes.

The second factor is, as Gilbert indicates, that British conservatism is in crisis. The pro-American consensus of British political life, summed up by the British politicians named in Gilbert's chapter, has stretched from the socialist left to conservative right. The extreme left and the extreme right, meanwhile, have always been anti-American and will not change. What has changed, however, is that the British right and center-right have become anti-American. Britain's Conservatives must now rank as one of the most xenophobic political movements in western Europe: They are anti-EU, anti-U.S., anti-immigrant, and, on occasion, anti-Irish. It is unclear who there is left for British Conservatives to hate.

Conservative anti-Americanism has resulted in American Republicans distancing themselves from the British Conservatives. Instead of being embarrassed about this, British Conservatives are so pleased that George W. Bush closed the door of the White House in then-Tory leader Michael Howard's face that they leaked the story to the British press.[14]

Third, the Labour Party's mismanagement of the Iraq issue has damaged the special relationship. Note that the problem is not the Iraq war in and of itself. Rather, the difficulty lies in the way that the government has handled criticisms of the war. Britain has been involved in other, less justified military operations without creating the same level of public controversy. The problem with Iraq is that Labour has simply ceded the issue to the antiwar movement and refused to debate it.

How much this failure cost Blair during the May 2005 general election is unclear. The conventional wisdom is that Iraq explains the loss of Labour seats during the general election.[15] However, a closer look at the results indicates that the Iraq effect was localized, and that there was no national trend during the elections. Labour held its two most vulnerable seats (Dumfries & Galloway and Dorset South) as well as Margaret Thatcher's old seat (Finchley & Golders Green). Yet Labour lost far safer seats such as Dumfriesshire, Clydesdale, and Tweeddale (their 80th most vulnerable seat and number 96 on the Conservatives' target list). They also lost Hornsey & Wood Green, a seat that the BBC considered so safe that it was not even listed as a target. Indeed, the Liberal Democrats, who ran an antiwar and anti-U.S. platform, were probably surprised to win Hornsey & Wood Green as it was only number 77 on their target list.[16] Local factors, such as tactical voting and an appeal to ethnic and religious prejudice, helped to hand the previously safe Labour seat of Bethnal Green & Bow to George Galloway, a former Labour Member of Parliament (MP) and apologist for Saddam Hussein.[17]

Of course, for all the talk of Labour being somehow damaged by the May 2005 general election, it is worth bearing in mind that Blair won a third consecutive term, a feat achieved before only by

Margaret Thatcher. Moreover, the size of Blair's three parliamentary majorities exceeds those achieved by Margaret Thatcher. Far from being a threat, the Conservatives won fewer seats in the 2005 elections than Labour did at its low point in the 1983 elections. For all the talk of Blair's leadership being threatened, it was the Conservative leader, Michael Howard, who resigned after the election. Blair has now put four Conservative leaders out of a job—not bad for a man whom the British media have repeatedly written off.

Conclusion and Recommendations.

What, then, should be done to inject new life and direction into the special relationship? Five policies need to be pursued.

First, the British government has to make the argument to its citizens that the special relationship serves Britain's distinct national interests. Many Britons do not like the idea of doing favors for foreigners, whether through EU subsidies or helping the United States feel less lonely as a superpower. Situating the special relationship within the context of EU-U.S. relations may win plaudits from policy wonks and editorial writers, but it is meaningless to the practical-minded British electorate. Instead, what the government should be explaining is that the special relationship gives Britain unprecedented leverage and access with the United States and, as importantly, in the EU and elsewhere. The reason why British Foreign Secretary Jack Straw was welcome in Iran in the months immediately following September 11, 2001, was that both Iran and the United States knew that he would be an honest intermediary. Both sides knew where they stood with this middleman. Such services could not have been rendered by France or Germany, given the French pursuit of its commercial interests with Iran and German contacts with Iranian intelligence.

For Britain, there is no need to make an exclusive choice between the EU and the United States. The dichotomy is false, since the EU is not a coherent bloc. What is often meant by the EU is nothing more than the Franco-German axis that claims to be the core of the EU. Were Britain to reduce its ties with the United States, there could well be important economic consequences and a humiliating reduction in British influence in the EU. The UK would be reduced to a third-rung power, a subsidiary of this Franco-German axis. On the other hand, were Britain to turn away from the EU, as Britain's Conservatives advocate, the damage to the British economy, and to Britain's influence on the continent, would be immense.

We need to understand that the problem for so many foreign, and in particular continental European, critics of the special relationship, is not its existence but its membership. Many EU states want to emulate Britain's close relations with the United States. Indeed, we can rest assured that if tomorrow Britain were to renounce the special relationship, the president of France would board the first flight to Washington, and hasten to the White House to press his claim to fill the spot vacated by Britain.

Second, the U.S.-British special relationship needs to demonstrate leadership across the spectrum of policy issues, not just security. If the special relationship is to matter, it must demonstrate leadership on precisely the economic and environmental issues which supposedly are its greatest weakness. A clear theme during the special relationship conference was the general failure of leadership on economic issues, with special reference to the complacent U.S. attitude toward its fiscal deficit and the unwillingness of the continental EU to pursue structural reform. The superficial thought in the EU regarding its economic future was neatly illustrated during the debate in France over the EU constitution. Chirac called neo-liberalism the new communism, and the only area of agreement during the referendum campaign was that both sides were hostile to the United States.

Blair challenged the continental critics of economic liberalism with his speech to the European Parliament on June 23, 2005, in which he pressed the EU for reform. The prime minister pointedly asked, "What type of social model is it that has 20 million unemployed in Europe."[18] It is an indication of how the continental EU is rethinking its approach to economic policy in the wake of the Franco-Dutch rejection of the EU constitution that the response to Blair's speech was so positive.[19] But Blair cannot defend free market economics on his own. George Bush must join him by demonstrating seriousness on the deficit. The President also needs to be more responsive to Blair's call for a global campaign of economic assistance to Africa.

The United States and the UK must also avoid easy solutions to complex economic and political problems exemplified by such long-standing proposals as a Transatlantic Free Trade Area (TAFTA) or the more recent call for a Global Free Trade Area (GAFTA). These schemes, to a degree, are designed to satisfy conservative ideology and its fetish for sovereignty (our sovereignty, nobody else's). To create such free trade arrangements would require destroying the EU single market, which conservatives dislike because it involves pooling sovereignty. Closing down the EU single market would, however, be too high a price for any British government to pay.

Britain also needs to lead the EU debate about the development of genuine security capabilities that complement rather than compete with the United States. At present, the EU is in the unfortunate position of being dependent upon Washington for its global security needs and unable to meaningfully contribute to its own defense. The result of this dependency is a climate of strategic irresponsibility in the EU. Again, Blair put it well on the eve of the Iraq war:

> I would never commit British troops to a war I thought was wrong or unnecessary. But the price of influence is that we do not leave the U.S. to face the tricky issues alone. By tricky, I mean the ones which people wish weren't there, don't want to deal with, and, if I can put it a little pejoratively, know the U.S. should confront, but want the luxury of criticising them for it.[20]

The luxury of criticism stems from the lack of capabilities of many EU states and their inability to come up with policy alternatives to U.S. proposals. The Franco-German position on Iraq boiled down to opposing the war in order to make the United States pay a high diplomatic price for changing a *status quo* that they had previously criticized. There was no expectation in either Paris or Berlin that diplomacy could resolve the issue of Iraqi noncompliance with UN Security Council resolutions, and both capitals accepted that war was inevitable. Their change of position was nothing more than posturing, without offering serious policy alternatives. As Jamie Rubin, the Clinton-era State Department spokesman, has observed, "After spending 1995 to 2000 criticizing Iraq sanctions, the Germans and French fell in love with containment."[21]

Third, the British government needs to privatize the state-owned news media. There is no need in a modern democracy for a state-owned broadcaster such as the BBC. The only reason why the BBC still exists is that the government controls its finances and so is able, from time to time, to prevent the BBC from broadcasting programs that it objects to. Margaret Thatcher engaged in this form of censorship on more than one occasion. Blair, meanwhile, has often found that this unrepresentative, state-financed media outlet has taken upon itself the mantle of the opposition to his government. He has tolerated this because he knows that during elections the left-leaning BBC will punish the Conservatives.

Such short-term political benefits have generated a longer-term political cost—consistent BBC bias against the United States and, in particular, the war against terrorism and the war in Iraq. The BBC has been particularly active in propagating the notion that the British and American governments misled their electorates to justify the war in Iraq—an extremely serious allegation that has been knocked down by repeated inquiries. The case for war has been twisted into a preemptive strike and a hunt for weapons of mass destruction (WMD) stocks in Iraq, when the motion put before the House of Commons on March 18, 2003, repeatedly mentioned Iraqi breaches of UN Security Council Resolutions and was legally based upon repeated Iraqi violations of the March 1991 Gulf War ceasefire.[22] The truly guilty party in distorting the case for the Iraq war was the BBC, as demonstrated by the Hutton inquiry which resulted in the resignation of the two top officials at the BBC, its chairman, Gavyn Davies, and its Director General, Greg Dyke. The journalist involved, Andrew Gilligan, also resigned and later joined a right-wing magazine that is edited by a Conservative MP, *The Spectator*. In a similar fashion, the BBC's astonishing response to the July 7, 2005, terrorist attacks in London illustrated just how unaccountable the organization had become. For hours the BBC stuck to the initial report that there had been an electrical "power surge" on the lines powering the London Underground railway. Once events finally forced the BBC to report that there had been a series of terrorist attacks, the corporation then struggled with calling such an attack on London "terrorism." Stories that initially used the words "terrorist" were subsequently edited to delete the word.[23]

Of course, the BBC's opinions are representative of a swathe of the educated class in London and the southeast, but they are not the opinions of the country, and they do not deserve to be funded by a form of regressive taxation. The unrepresentative nature of these views is encapsulated in the standard term used about the BBC and similar self-styled opinion formers — the "chattering classes."

Fourth, the United States must clarify its attitude towards international law and, in particular, torture. The perception that the United States wants international law *à la carte* is extremely damaging both to U.S. influence and to the legitimacy of the war against terrorism. Allegations, in some cases well-founded, of torture of detainees need to be fully addressed. Above all, the U.S. government needs to distance itself from those on the left and the right who are willing to countenance torture,[24] and instead articulate a principled opposition to torture because it is morally wrong and damaging to any serious prosecution of the war against terrorism.[25]

None of this means that the United States should bow to the new pseudo-legalism of human rights groups. The human rights industry consistently holds the United States and its allies to higher standards than the rest of the world and seeks to confound efforts by democracies to defend themselves against aggression and terrorism.[26]

One argument put forward during the special relationship conference and mentioned by Philip Stephens in the sessions in both the United States and the UK bears some similarity to the unrealistic arguments of members of the human rights community. Stephens argued that no British prime minister could go to war again in support of the United States without UN backing. If Stephens had confined himself to saying that another Iraq-style venture was not politically feasible under present circumstances, then his judgment would have been correct. But his claim was broader and worrisome, implying as it did that a somehow chastened Britain could not risk taking assertive action abroad without the sanction of some ideal "international community." Such a standard would unfairly tie Britain's hands and its ability to defend itself. We cannot foresee future contingencies, and the right to use force in self-defense is a right recognized, not granted, by article 51 of the UN charter. It is interesting to note that when John Kerry suggested that any contemplated U.S. preemptive action should pass a "global test" of convincing the rest of the world of its justification,[27] he was pounced on by critics.[28] What Stephens is proposing resembles the right-wing caricature of Kerry's comments, a surrender of British sovereignty to the UN Security Council.

Fifth, Washington and London should continue to lead the battle against Islamist terrorism and Ba'athism, but they must do a better job of explaining that these wars are not elective. They must also present a more convincing case for a long-term political, military, and economic commitment to Iraq. To leave early, allowing Iraq's nascent democracy to fail, would be to betray the Iraqis yet again and to nullify the value of either Britain or the United States as an ally.

The war against Islamist extremism requires a careful melding of political and security measures. The battle for public opinion is an important aspect of the battle against the jihadists. Too often, however, Britain and the United States have defined the war in negative, defensive terms, for example, that it is not a war against Islam.[29] Constantly on the back foot, they have failed to define what they are fighting for. Bush's inaugural address and State of the Union speech in 2005 were sweeping renunciations of the *realpolitik* practiced by his father.[30] While Bush may think he is a conservative, his foreign policy is consistent with Blair's vision of an ethical foreign policy and of a global community. In his willingness to shake up the existing world order, Bush's policy carries strong echoes of the British left's long-standing hostility to dictatorships and states that imprison unwilling populations. Blair's speech following the London bombings, which echoed his comments to the Labour Party conference in 2004,[31] began to address this deficit by pointing out that there can be no compromise or policy changes that will assuage the jihadists.[32]

Still, more needs to be done.[33] A world without terrorism should be our goal, but even for a world that often does not feel threatened by terrorism there needs to be more to offer. The promises of democracy without development and of globalization without global economic justice are not particularly appetizing. By contrast, Britain and the United States should pledge that more open societies will benefit from more open trade relations, and that there will be tangible economic benefits to societies that curb terrorism and extremism. Articulating a vision of how the world can look after the defeat of

Islamist terrorism and Ba'athism will not convince all the skeptics, but it will force them to come up with their own alternatives.

ENDNOTES - CHAPTER 7

1. Christopher Hitchens, *Blood, Class and Empire: The Enduring Anglo-American Relationship* (2nd Ed.), New York, 2004, pp. 118-119.

2. John Gooch, "The Weary Titan: Strategy and Policy in Great Britain, 1890-1918," in Williamson Murray, MacGregor Knox, and Alvin Bernstein, eds., *The Making of Strategy: Rulers, States and War*, Cambridge, 1994, p. 289.

3. Laila Freivalds, Minister for Foreign Affairs, and Carin Jämtin, Minister for International Development Cooperation, "Darfur Must be Treated as Genocide," Ministry for Foreign Affairs, August 6, 2004, available at *http://www.sweden.gov.se/sb/d/3308/a/28085*, last accessed July 17, 2005.

4. United Nations, *Report of the International Commission of Inquiry on Darfur to the United Nations Secretary-General Pursuant to Security Council Resolution 1564 of September 18, 2004*, Geneva, January 25, 2005, available at *http://www.un.org/News/dh/sudan/com_inq_darfur.pdf*, last accessed July 17, 2005.

5. He then argues as follows:

> Foreigners tend also not to understand why the U.S. is so reluctant to join in these international efforts. They know that many now democratic countries owe their freedom to international efforts and to the human rights support provided by international organizations. And they also believe that without external assistance they would not have been able to escape from under the oppressive rule of military governments or dictatorial civilian regimes that were in power in their countries. Moreover, the people who live in countries where such regimes still hold sway, have little faith in the willingness or capacity of their national judicial and political institutions to protect their human rights without strong international pressure.

Thomas Buergenthal, *International Law and the Holocaust*, Joseph and Rebecca Meyerhoff Annual Lecture, October 28, 2003, U.S. Holocaust Memorial Museum, Washington, DC, 2004, p. 24, available at *http://www.ushmm.org/research/center/publications/occasional/2003-10-28/paper.pdf*, last accessed July 17, 2005. Buergenthal was born in Czechoslovakia and survived the Holocaust.

6. Ferdinand Mount, "Blair's Back—Could His Current Kudos Persuade Him Not To Go?" *The Daily Telegraph*, July 13, 2005, available at *http://www.telegraph.co.uk/opinion/main.jhtml?xml=/opinion/2005/07/13/do1301.xml&sSheet=/portal/2005/07/13/ixportal.html*, last accessed July 17, 2005.

7. Peter Stothard, *Thirty Days: An Inside Account of Tony Blair at War*, London, 2004, contains numerous details on this.

8. Andrew Rawnsley, "The Lame Duck is Flying Again: The Hunted Prime Minister of the Election Campaign has been Transformed into a Man Back in Charge of the Agenda," *The Observer*, June 26, 2005, available at *http://observer.guardian.co.uk/comment/story/0,6903,1514798,00.html*, last accessed July 17, 2005.

9. Commission on Presidential Debates, "The First Bush-Kerry Presidential Debate," September 30, 2004, available at *http://www.debates.org/pp./trans2004a.html*, last accessed July 17, 2005.

10. "Bush, Blair Discuss Sharon Plan; Future of Iraq in Press Conference," Remarks by the President and United Kingdom Prime Minister Tony Blair in Rose Garden, available at *http://www.whitehouse.gov/news/releases/2004/04/20040416-4.html*, last accessed July 17, 2005.

11. Paul Routledge, chief political commentator, "Premier Creeps to Texan Idiot," *The Daily Mirror*, April 17, 2004, available at *http://www.mirror.co.uk/news/allnews/tm_objectid=14154586&method=full&siteid=50143&headline=premiercreep s-to-eejit-texan-name_p..html*, last accessed June 26, 2005. The same newspaper declared the day after the U.S. presidential elections "DOH! 4 MORE YEARS OF DUBYA. How can 59,054,087 people be so DUMB?" See June Thomas, "Brits to America: You're Idiots! Well, 51 percent of you, anyway," *Slate*, November 4, 2004, available at *http://slate.msn.com/id/2109242/*, last accessed July 17, 2005.

12. Pew Global Attitudes Project, "U.S. Image Up Slightly, But Still Negative: American Character Gets Mixed Reviews" Released June 23, 2005, available at *http://pewglobal.org/reports/display.php?ReportID=247*, last accessed July 17, 2005.

13. Anne Applebaum, "In Search of Pro-Americanism," *Foreign Policy*, July/August 2005, available at *http://www.foreignpolicy.com/story/cms.php?story_id=3080&p.=0*, last accessed July 1, 2005.

14. Trevor Kavanagh, "Bush: Stay away Howard," *The Sun*, August 28, 2004.

15. Nick Assinder, "Iraq hit Blair hard," *BBC News website*, May 7, 2005, available at: *http://news.bbc.co.uk/1/hi/uk_politics/vote_2005/frontp./4521337.stm*, last accessed July 17, 2005.

16. "BBC, Labour Defence and Targets," May 23, 2005, available at h*ttp://news.bbc.co.uk/1/shared/vote2005/html/gainsandlosses_lab.stm#target*, last accessed July 17, 2005.

17. Jenny Booth, "Oona King Reveals 'yid' Taunts During Election," *The Times*, London, May 11, 2005, available at *http://www.timesonline.co.uk/article/0,,2-1607947,00.html*, last accessed July 17, 2005.

18. PM speech to EU Parliament: full text, June 23, 2005, available at *http://www.number10.gov.uk/output/P.7714.asp*, last accessed July 17, 2005.

19. George Parker and Raphael Minder in Brussels and John Thornhill in Paris, "Blair's vision for Europe Wins Praise of MEPs," *The Financial Times*, June 24, 2005, available at *http://news.ft.com/cms/s/63fe774c-e44c-11d9-a754-00000e2511c8.html*, last accessed July 17, 2005.

20. Michael White and Ewen MacAskill, "Listen to the World's Fears, Blair Tells US," *The Guardian*, January 8, 2003, available at *http://www.guardian.co.uk/ Iraq/Story/0,2763,870491,00.html*, last accessed July 17, 2005. Put equally bluntly by Thérèse Delpech, "Insecurity has globalised, and a global vision as well as global cooperation are needed to meet the threat Today, Europe lacks both," *International terrorism and Europe*, Chaillot Paper 56, December 2002, p. 49, available at *http:// www.iss-eu.org/chaillot/chai56e.pdf*, last accessed July 17, 2005.

21. David Rieff, "Were Sanctions Right?" *The New York Times*, Sec. 6; Col. 3; Magazine Desk; July 27, 2003, available at *http://www.globalpolicy.org/security/ sanction/iraq1/2003/0727right.htm*, last accessed July 17, 2005.

22. "Motion to Approve the Actions of Her Majesty's Government on Iraq," available at *http://www.publications.parliament.uk/pa/cm200203/cmhansrd/vo030318/ debtext/30318-06.htm#30318-06_head1*. The full debate is in *Hansard*, HC Deb 401 c760-911.

23. Gene Zitver, "The BBC's 'Terrorist' Problem," *Harry's Place*, July 8, 2005, available at *http://hurryupharry.bloghouse.net/archives/2005/07/08/the_bbcs_terrorist_ problem.php*, last accessed July 17, 2005. A BBC story on July 7, 2005, had the headline "Bus Man may have seen Terrorist," and the opening paragraph stated, "A bus passenger says he may have seen one of those responsible for the terrorist bomb attacks in London." By July 8, 2005, the headline had been altered to "Passenger believes he saw bomber," and the word "terrorist" had been excised from the article. Another article on the morning of July 8, 2005, which referred to "the worst terrorist atrocity Britain has seen" was altered within hours to "the worst peacetime bomb attacks Britain has seen." Zitver's analysis was picked up in *The Times*, London. See Daniel Finkelstein, "Politeness in the Photocopier Queue Is Why We're Losing the War on Terror," *The Times*, July 13, 2005, available at *http:// www.timesonline.co.uk/article/0,,21129-1691644,00.html*, last accessed July 17, 2005.

24. Andrew C. McCarthy, "Torture: Thinking About the Unthinkable," *Commentary*, Vol. 118, No. 1, July 2004, available at *http://www.benadorassociates. com/article/5900*, last accessed July 17, 2005; Phillip Carter, "The Road to Abu Ghraib, the Biggest Scandal of the Bush administration, Began at the Top," *The Washington Monthly*, November 2004, available at *http://www.washingtonmonthly. com/features/2004/0411.carter.html*, last accessed July 17, 2005.

25. Anne Applebaum, "So Torture Is Legal?" *The Washington Post*, June 16, 2004, p. A27, available at *http://www.washingtonpost.com/wp-dyn/articles/A44874- 2004Jun15.html*; "The Torture Myth," *The Washington Post*, January 12, 2005, p. A21, available at *http://www.washingtonpost.com/wp-dyn/articles/A2302-2005Jan11. html*, last accessed July 17, 2005.

26. John Keegan, "Bad Law Is Making a Just War So Much Harder to Fight," *The Daily Telegraph*, June 2, 2005, available at *http://www.opinion.telegraph.co.uk/opinion/ main.jhtml?xml=/opinion/2005/06/02/do0201.xml&sSheet=/opinion/2005/06/02/ ixopinion.html*, last accessed July 17, 2005.

27. Commission on Presidential Debates, "The First Bush-Kerry Presidential Debate," September 30, 2004, available at *http://www.debates.org/pp./trans2004a.html*, last accessed July 17, 2005.

28. Lee A. Casey and David B. Rivkin, Jr., "Kerry's 'global' test," *The Washington Times*, October 8, 2004, available at *http://washingtontimes.com/op-ed/20041007-092532-8329r.htm*, last accessed July 17, 2005.

29. Andrew Apostolou, "The War of Ideas," *The New York Post*, November 8, 2001.

30. Bush had already publicly renounced *realpolitik* in his speech to the National Endowment for Democracy. "President Bush Discusses Freedom in Iraq and Middle East," Remarks by the President at the 20th Anniversary of the National Endowment for Democracy; United States Chamber of Commerce, Washington, DC, November 6, 2003, available at *http://www.whitehouse.gov/news/releases/2003/11/20031106-2.html*, last accessed July 17, 2005.

31. Blair speech to Labour Party conference, September 28, 2005, available at *http://news.bbc.co.uk/1/hi/uk_politics/3697434.stm*, last accessed July 17, 2005.

32. Blair speech to the Labour Party's national policy forum, July 16, 2005, available at *http://news.bbc.co.uk/1/hi/uk/4689363.stm*, last accessed July 17, 2005. Consider, for example, the following excerpt:

> The extremist propaganda is cleverly aimed at their target audience. It plays on our tolerance and good nature. It exploits the tendency to guilt of the developed world, as if it is our behaviour that should change, that if we only tried to work out and act on their grievances, we could lift this evil, that if we changed our behaviour, they would change theirs. This is a misunderstanding of a catastrophic order.

SECTION III:

FOREIGN POLICY AND THE SPECIAL RELATIONSHIP

CHAPTER 8

A CONSERVATIVE VISION
FOR U.S. POLICY TOWARD EUROPE

John C. Hulsman and Nile Gardiner

The United Kingdom (UK) is likely to remain America's paramount ally for the foreseeable future. That is why it is in America's fundamental national interest to assist Britain to continue playing this pivotal role. Washington's management of its relationship with the European Union (EU) will be a key determinant of the UK's ability to maintain its influence and options as a global and regional actor.

Since joining the then European Community in 1973, Britain has had an uneasy and sometimes tumultuous relationship with its European partners. During this period, the EU has evolved from a largely economic grouping of nation-states into an inward-looking political entity, with ever-greater political centralization. The British have found their national sovereignty gradually eroded by EU laws and regulations.

Despite efforts by British Prime Minister Tony Blair to play a leading role in Europe, the British public has grown increasingly disillusioned with EU membership in the past few years. In a recent Institute of Commercial Management (ICM) poll commissioned by the New Frontiers Foundation, 59 percent of Britons agreed with the suggestion that the UK "should take back powers from the EU and develop a new global trade and defense alliance with America, some in Europe, and other countries across the world." Just 30 percent of respondents said that Britain "should join the Euro and Constitution and aim for a political union in Europe."

The UK's future direction in Europe will directly impact the United States. Economically, it is hard to imagine how two countries could be closer. Between 1995 and 2003, 64 percent of total U.S. direct investment in the EU went to the UK, while 62 percent of EU investment in the United States originated in Britain. The United States and the UK easily remain the largest foreign direct investors in each other's economies. These extraordinarily close financial ties between the world's largest and fourth largest economies would alone make the UK a primary U.S. national security interest.

Militarily, along with France and the United States, the UK is one of only three North Atlantic Treaty Organization (NATO) powers capable of sustaining a global military presence in terms of both transport capacity and logistics. It is unfortunate that Britain is embarking on major cuts in its armed forces as part of a modernization program. While supposedly improving Britain's niche in military capabilities, the cuts are likely to leave the British military severely overstretched.

Nevertheless, these three powers are the only Atlantic allies that can participate in the entire military spectrum, from high-end, technologically intricate major warfighting through low-end peacekeeping. It is also helpful that both France and the UK are the only European countries with a genuine geopolitical grasp of military realities (partly due to their colonial histories) and a political tolerance for casualties. This state of affairs is not expected to change—it is highly unlikely that any other NATO power will obtain a significant global reach in the medium term.

Perhaps the single greatest asset accruing to the United States from its relationship with Britain, however, is the UK's proven political slant toward America. The two countries have a unique, long-standing tradition of working intimately with one another, as demonstrated in World Wars I and II, the Cold War, Afghanistan, Iraq, and the fight against al-Qaeda. This ingrained affinity—the product of a common cultural heritage, a common commitment to free markets and free elections, and common geopolitical views—is without parallel in the world. It explains why the UK is currently so vital to U.S. coalition-building and is likely to remain so.

But this relationship obscures fairy tales America has told itself about the EU. For the past half-century, the policymaking elite in Washington has come to similarly positive conclusions about America's relations with Europe at large: every effort at closer European integration is to be welcomed, if tepidly. The assumption has been that a unified Europe would inevitably prove more pro-free market, more pro-Atlanticist, and more pro-American. Today, however, following the transatlantic rift over the Iraq war and the public diplomacy calamity that has ensued for the United States, such simplistic analysis is starkly at odds with the schism at the heart of the post–Cold War transatlantic relationship.

The United States should stop merely reacting to fundamental changes in Europe, voicing platitudes from the sidelines, and adopt a more proactive approach. Washington should develop a series of strategic, diplomatic, and analytical principles, with political, economic, and military dimensions, to guide its policies toward NATO and the EU and its plans for reviving the transatlantic relationship. In formulating these principles, the United States should follow the conservative precepts of the great 18th century British statesman, Edmund Burke, who insisted on seeing the world as it is, not as some might hope it to be.

The first principle should be recognition of the continuing strategic centrality of Europe. Whatever the global issue—be it the war on al-Qaeda, the Doha trade round, Iran's efforts to develop weapons of mass destruction (WMD), the Arab-Israeli conflict, or the future of Iraq—the United States simply cannot act effectively without the support of at least some European powers. The United States remains first among equals, but the world is neither genuinely unipolar nor multipolar, which makes it vital for America to continue to court allies. For the foreseeable future, there will be only one place to find those allies—Europe. It is the sole area of the world where political, diplomatic, military, and economic power can be generated in sufficient strength to support American policies effectively. The cluster of international powers in Europe—led by the United Kingdom, France, Germany, Italy, Spain, and Poland—has no parallel.

The leading European nations, however, rarely agree on most of today's key issues of foreign and security policy. As a result, the United States must engage European states on an issue-by-issue, case-by-case basis to gain the greatest number of allies for the largest number of missions, thus maximizing its diplomatic effectiveness.

The second principle that should drive American policy toward Europe centers on the importance of national choice and sovereignty. American interests are best served when European states act flexibly according to their separate interests, rather than collectively according to some utopian ideal. Although the day may be far off, an

EU implementing a genuinely supranational common foreign and security policy could clearly hamstring American efforts to form political, military, or economic coalitions with individual member countries.

To illustrate the point, one need only look at the EU common commercial policy, under which the European Commission conducts international negotiations on behalf of the EU. Since the member states have not reached a consensus on the very principle of free trade, the EU formulates trade policy on the basis of the lowest common denominator. It can proceed only as fast as its most protectionist member allows. This adherence to supranationalism keeps largely free-trading nations with more open economies—such as the UK, Ireland, Denmark, Sweden, Finland, the Netherlands, and Estonia—from following their sovereign interests and developing closer and mutually beneficial trading ties with the United States.

This one-size-fits-all approach does not comport well with the political realities of the continent today. European countries have politically diverse opinions on all aspects of international life: free trade, NATO, relations with the United States, and how to organize their own economies. Ireland, for example, is a strong free-trading country, has extensive ties to the United States, and favors a large degree of economic liberalization. France, by contrast, is more protectionist, more statist in organizing its economy, and more competitive in its attitude toward America. Germany falls between the two on free trade and relations with the United States, but favors some liberalization of its economy to retain its corporatist model. Strategically, Ireland is neutral, France is inherently hostile to NATO, while Germany is more pro-NATO than France but prefers UN involvement in crises over that of the alliance. Such real European diversity ought to be reflected in each state's control over its foreign and security policy. A more centralized Europe simply does not reflect the political reality on the ground.

Third, the United States must follow Burke's advice and see Europe as it is, not as some Europeans might wish it. Europe collectively is far weaker than its federalist adherents proclaim. Simply put, it is considerably less than the sum of its parts. In the wake of the Iraq war, the EU looks economically sclerotic, militarily weak, and politically disunited.

Economically, the Franco-German-Italian core of the Eurozone has structurally high unemployment. Staggeringly, according to the Organization for Economic Cooperation and Development (OECD), between 1970 and 2000 the 12 countries now in the Euro area did not create any net private sector jobs. The demographic problems created by Europe's falling birthrate and aging population—linked to its over-generous social safety net—make the preservation of its way of life highly dubious in the medium-term without radical reform. Unless Europe as a whole deals with this massive problem, it will be consigned to the status of an elderly theme park.

Militarily, the collective picture is also grim. Despite a market that is slightly larger than that of the United States, European defense spending is two-thirds that of the United States and fields only 20 percent of the fighting strength that American can deploy. Even the current level of spending and capability is in peril. In the words of leading American defense expert Richard Perle, Europe's armed forces have already "atrophied to the point of virtual irrelevance."

Politically, Europeans remain deeply divided on seminal issues of war and peace, as demonstrated by the fundamental differences between Britain and France and Germany over Iraq. The basic reason is that national interests still dominate foreign policy-making at the most critical moments, even for states ostensibly committed to common foreign and security policies. For the European powers, Iraq has never been primarily about Iraq. It is about the attitudes of Europeans toward post-Cold War American power and their jockeying for position within common European institutions.

One camp, championed by France, is distrustful of American power and strives to create a centralized EU as a rival pole of power to America. The other camp, led by Britain and including the Scandinavian, Baltic, and Central and Eastern European states, seeks to engage American power and favors a more decentralized Union. This very disparate political, economic, and military picture of Europe explains why the EU constitution—the latest attempt to impose greater central control over the European process—has been rejected by the voters in both France and the Netherlands. There is no doubt that the framers of the European project started with over-lofty goals, to the extent of making false comparisons with the drafting of the U.S. Constitution in Philadelphia in 1787.

According to the Laeken Declaration of December 2001, which launched the process of replacing the Union's existing treaties, the new European document was supposed to clarify the division of competencies among the EU institutions, the member states, and the people, making the Union more efficient and open. The institutions were to be brought closer to Europe's citizens in an effort to lessen the Union's "democratic deficit." This was to be a two-way process, with some powers returned to the member states and the people and some new competencies bestowed on Brussels. These high hopes bear little resemblance to the finished product. In fact, the document was riven with contradictions, many of which were to be worked out over time by the European Court of Justice, with "ever-closer union" as its mandate. This scheme can readily be seen as an effort at further centralization through the back door, a result wholly out of line with the notion of a diverse Europe. Tellingly, the constitution did little to provide citizens with a sense of control over the process of European government or the evolution of the Union.

These egregious flaws explain why the constitutional referendum was soundly defeated by French and Dutch citizens. Indeed, these voters did other European governments a favor by killing the treaty before they were forced to confront ratification. American policymakers must now accept that the EU drive toward ever-closer union has at last decisively sputtered, and that engaging Europeans at the state level generally will be far more effective than engaging the EU itself.

Given these broad principles, the United States should advance the following policies toward Europe. First, Washington should favor a multispeed Europe, with each state having greater choice about its level of integration. It now seems possible that France will make the case for the creation of a more integrated, confederal European core dominated by France and Germany, with Italy, Belgium, and Luxembourg as probable members. The United States should accept this possible initiative since it will contribute to the development of a genuinely multispeed Europe. But the French cannot be the only ones to redefine their role. There must be at least two speeds to a reconstituted EU: the inner core, a group of states that wish to remain roughly as integrated as they are now, and an outer core that wants looser ties with Brussels. This latter group ought to regain the right to join trading blocs with non-EU countries. This will require a trade opt-out, just as a new confederal opt-in will be necessary for the inner core.

Such a reconstituted process must be negotiated all at once, so that the newly defined inner core, led by France as described above, cannot stop other states from also altering their relationship with the EU. If such a policy is adopted, individual European states will be free to decide their own destinies.

Second, the United States must launch a massive public diplomacy campaign in Europe if it is to retain the ability to engage European countries as allies. There is little doubt that the conflicts over the war in Iraq and its aftermath have been a diplomatic disaster of the first magnitude for Washington. While many European governments still support U.S. policy in Iraq, the general public remains extremely hostile to American foreign policy. The recently published Gallup transatlantic Trends 2004 poll of opinion in nine major EU countries found that 58 percent of European respondents believed that strong U.S. leadership in the world was "undesirable."

If Europe is the most likely place for America to find allies well into the new century, it must become the main focus of U.S. global efforts at public diplomacy. Fostering goodwill toward America will make a greater practical difference in Europe than anywhere else in the world. It may take a generation to rejuvenate the transatlantic alliance, and America must not underestimate the scale of the problem if this new strategy is to work. But unless public diplomacy is used effectively, America may have no European allies in the future.

Third, the United States should help establish a Global Free Trade Alliance (GFTA), opening the door to genuine free trade with qualified European nations in the outer core. A GFTA would be an economic coalition of the willing, determined to liberalize trade among its members, augmenting already existing bilateral, regional, and multilateral free trade negotiations. It would not be a treaty but a legislative initiative, offering free trade between the United States and other nations with a demonstrable commitment to free trade and investment, minimal regulation, and property rights. Congress would offer GFTA members access to the U.S. market, with no tariffs, quotas, or other trade barriers, on the single condition that they offer the same access to the United States and other members of the group.

The GFTA would associate the United States and genuine free-trading European nations with other dynamic economies around the world, such as Australia, Hong Kong, New Zealand, and Singapore. The GFTA would have no standing secretariat, and institutional cooperation would be limited to formal meetings of the member countries' trade ministers, staffs, and technical experts. Further decisions on trading initiatives — such as codifying uniform standards on subsidies and capital flows — would be made on a consensual basis to further minimize barriers within the alliance.

A GFTA could change the way people and countries think about free trade. Further global trade liberalization would no longer require wrangling over "concessions." Instead, free trade would be seen for what it is, a policy that gives countries a massive economic advantage. As the benefits of the alliance become apparent, the GFTA would serve as a practical advertisement for global free trade. Such an organization would be extremely attractive to the outer European core, who are tired of the overly statist strictures of protectionist Brussels. And Britain would be America's natural ally in the sponsorship of this initiative.

Fourth, the United States should continue to press for NATO reform, particularly through increased use of the Combined Joint Task Force (CJTF) mechanism, endorsed by NATO governments in April 1999. Until recently, the alliance could take on a mission only if all its members agreed to do so. Under CJTF procedures, NATO member states do not have to participate actively in a mission if they do not feel their vital interests are at stake, but their absence does not stop other members from going ahead. As Iraq illustrates, there are almost always some allies who will go along with any specific American policy initiative.

The new *modus operandi* would work both ways. Sometimes the United States would act together with those allies that wanted to join it; sometimes European countries would act without the United States. In fact, the first *de facto* use of the new procedure involved European efforts to head off civil conflict in Macedonia. The United States wisely noted that Macedonia was, to put it mildly, not a primary national interest. For Italy, however, with the Adriatic as its Rio Grande, upheaval in Macedonia would have had serious consequences, destabilizing a nearby region and causing an unwanted flow of refugees. By allowing a group of European states to use common NATO facilities — such as logistics, lift, and intelligence capabilities, most of which were American in origin — while refraining from putting U.S. boots on the ground, Washington followed a sensible middle course that averted a crisis in the alliance.

Beyond the sacrosanct Article V commitment, which holds that an attack on one alliance member is an assault on all, the future of NATO consists of just these sorts of "coalitions of the willing" acting out of area. Such operations are likely to become the norm in an era of a politically fragmented Europe. The United States should call for full NATO consultation on almost every major politico-military issue of the day. If full NATO support is not forthcoming, Washington should doggedly pursue the diplomatic dance, rather than treating such a rebuff as the end of the process, as many strict multilateralists would counsel.

If action by a subset of the alliance proved impossible, owing to a general blocking of such an initiative, the United States should form a coalition of willing countries around the globe outside NATO. After exhausting these options. America should be prepared to act alone if fundamental national interests are at stake.

Fifth, the United States must continue to encourage European members of NATO to modernize the alliance by developing a rapid reaction force — quickly deployable, highly lethal, and expeditionary — so as not to erode the sharing of risks that is so vital to the continued functioning of the organization.

The present unequal division of labor between the United States and its European allies — with the United States fighting the wars and the Europeans keeping the peace — sets an awful precedent for the future of the alliance. France and Britain apart, Europe's paltry military spending means that the continent's only hope of making a viable contribution to allied security is to modernize and pool resources, in an effort to play niche roles in an overall American-led defense strategy.

There is also a vast and growing technological discrepancy, with the United States spending nearly four times more than its European allies on defense research and development. Barely 10 percent of Western Europe's 5,000 attack aircraft, for example, are capable of precision bombing, and Europe has almost no independent "lift" capacity to transport an army at will. If the United States continues to be the "mercenary" of the alliance while the Europeans are the "social workers," this functional disparity will lead to constant differences in political views and imperil the viability of the alliance.

Sixth, the United States should continue to realign and update its European base structure to meet the challenges of the 21st century. President George W. Bush has called for the removal of up to 70,000 U.S. troops from Europe and Asia over 10 years, in a sweeping reorganization that would better prepare the armed forces to handle post–September 11, 2001, crises. Two armored divisions would return to the United States from Germany and be replaced by one light-armored brigade. The plan calls for more troops to be deployed farther south and east in Europe, nearer the arc of instability (the Caucasus, Iraq, Iran, the Middle East, and North Africa), where future crises are most likely to originate.

This redeployment is more consistent with the realities of today's threats and will help to remedy NATO's current inability to deploy troops quickly. By making more American troops ready for rapid deployment, the United States will help to revitalize the alliance and increase its relevance to today's problems.

The restructuring will also increase America's geostrategic flexibility. The United States currently is too dependent on a few vital NATO countries. Developing a presence in other European nations will spread the strategic risk and decrease America's dependence on any one NATO ally. Turkey, for example, will no longer be one of the few critical pressure points in mounting a military campaign in the Middle East, as it was during preparations for the war in Iraq. American bases in Bulgaria and Romania would shift some of the burden away from this hard-pressed ally, allowing Ankara to emphasize military action as regional in nature, not solely as a make-or-break U.S.-Turkish matter.

It is also important to emphasize that any removal of American forces from Germany is not a reaction to Berlin's opposition to the war in Iraq. It is imperative to reaffirm that Washington values its traditional European alliances, especially with Germany, and that the restructuring efforts will benefit all of Europe by adjusting NATO's force structure to reflect the fact that the world has entered a different era.

Conclusion.

Only by grounding American policy prescriptions in a new view of Europe will it prove possible to escape from the reactive nature of current American efforts to deal with the bewildering continent. By following Burke's adage, it becomes clear that "Europe" is less than its admirers claim and more than its detractors admit. European countries remain the foundation of all coalitions that America can assemble well into the future, with the UK playing a critical role. It is also true that the United States simply cannot act effectively in the world without at least some European allies, whatever the issue. Furthermore, Europe is not the monolith bloc to which EU integrationists aspire. On the contrary, it shows amazing diversity, whether the issues are economic, military, or political. Europe is ultimately a hodgepodge, and this perfectly suits American interests.

Simply put, America will be able to engage European governments most successfully in a Europe in which national sovereignty remains paramount in foreign and security policy, and in which states act flexibly rather than collectively. This flexibility, whether in international institutions or in ad hoc coalitions of the willing, is the future of the transatlantic relationship, for it fits the objective realities of the state of the continent. Such a Europe is worth conserving.

CHAPTER 9

PAST, PRESENT, AND FUTURE FOREIGN POLICY:
THE BRITISH PERSPECTIVE

Nicholas Childs

A foreign policy guide to the special relationship is in some ways simple for anyone in Britain: Acknowledge its existence and inevitability, based on an amalgam of cultural, linguistic, economic, and emotional ties unmatched by any other partner of the United States. These factors encourage both Washington and London to cooperate on almost all the big questions. As the world's dominant power, America will have "special relations" with many countries: Russia, China, and Israel. But not like this one. That is why, fundamentally, it is impossible to see Britain joining any camp that views the United States as a strategic rival rather than a strategic collaborator. And that is why, even when there is a falling out between Washington and London, it is still different from the way it would be with any other countries.

But also accept that at times this can be a difficult, unrewarding, and unforgiving affair between two sovereign nations of vastly different weight, with different national interests. In the military and strategic jargon of our time, it is very "asymmetric." But it was almost ever thus. I recall the uneasy smile on the face of President George W. Bush when the then visiting North Atlantic Treaty Organization (NATO) Secretary-General Lord Robertson paused by a bust of Winston Churchill in the White House (surely the fact that it is there at all speaks volumes) and recalled the great Prime Minister's wry observation — which surely captures the essence of the issue — that the Americans can always be relied upon to do the right thing, once they have exhausted all other possibilities. Fundamentally, the Americans and the British agree on what is right and important. But, as the Cunard Company claimed when its great Anglo-American ambassadors, the liners *Queen Mary* and *Queen Elizabeth*, used to surge across the ocean creating their own transatlantic bridge: "Getting there is half the fun."

There is no getting away from the fact that the United States is the most powerful nation in the world by a huge margin. So it can be tough on friend and foe alike if it chooses. But within limits. While America may never have been so strong, and while globalization and the information revolution may mean that the planet has never seemed so small, it is also true that the international community has never been so unwieldy and willful, the levers of diplomacy so weak, and the costs of exerting real influence apparently so high. For these reasons, Washington must as a first resort invariably seek friends and allies. Then too, there is in Britain, in Whitehall, in the British news media, and sometimes among the population as well, a wish to be loved and appreciated. But, especially when the relationship is as lopsided as this one, there has got to be something in it for both sides.

Of course, history is full of tensions and frictions in the relationship. The irony in this relationship is that, most often, it has been most influential when it has been most controversial. Think how difficult it was for President Franklin Roosevelt to extend a hand to Britain in the aftermath of the fall of France, and before Pearl Harbor? The heydays of the Thatcher-Reagan double-act were also some of the stormiest in terms of transatlantic tensions during the Cold War, with difficult and controversial choices for the British government, in particular, to make. These were the years of the cruise missile and *Pershing* ballistic missile deployments, Britain's active support for the U.S. bombing of Libya, the Reagan-Weinberger arms build-up, and the Reagan fulminations against "the evil empire" of the Soviet Union. We can look back on each of these periods with a measure of historical perspective. We know the significance of the outcome: the successful partnership in World War II and the beginning of the end of the Cold War. In the current situation, however, we do not have the luxury of critical distance, and Washington and London must manage their relationship in the highly toxic environment existent since the invasion of Iraq. Clearly, the occupation and reconstruction of Iraq has cost much more in terms of lives and treasure than had been expected, at least by those who were making the political decisions. The insurgency is far from defeated. What will emerge from the political fluidity created in the region as a whole is very uncertain. It could all look very different from the vantage point of 2015, but we cannot tell yet.

The other immediate challenge is that the traditional mainstays of the special relationship have been military power and intelligence collaboration, currencies in which Britain has still had a relatively significant amount in the bank, and ones that carried particular value during the Cold War. But they are precisely the ones whose value and credibility have been most called into question as a result of Iraq.

On the military front, the close cooperation between the Pentagon and the Ministry of Defence in the run-up to war with Iraq was clear from my vantage point as the BBC correspondent at the Pentagon. U.S. defense officials always made it clear that if they had to do the major combat operation on their own, they could. And, indeed, we learned from Robert Woodward's book, *Plan of Attack*, that that option was explicitly offered to Tony Blair because of his domestic political difficulties.[1] That is not to diminish the respect in which the British military is clearly held in the Pentagon. Without the British joining in at that stage, an already complex and finely-judged military plan would probably have been complicated still further, with even more serious consequences for the post-conflict phase.

But 2 years after the invasion, as much as it is a symbol of the U.S.-UK military alliance, Iraq is a reminder of the limits of conventional military power and a lesson, even for the United States, that military power is not a limitless resource. The Americans have just under 140,000 personnel in Iraq, and will probably have a significant fraction of that number there for several years.

Britain, for its part, has around 8,000 personnel still committed in its sector of Iraq. And the bottom line is that, whatever they say, both militaries are highly circumscribed in what they can and cannot now contemplate in terms of additional commitments, with the inevitable policy consequences. The Ministry of Defence has been more open in acknowledging that the British armed forces will not be in a position to replicate Operation IRAQI FREEDOM for several years. The recently departed Chairman of the U.S. Joint Chiefs of Staff, General Richard Myers, candidly acknowledged that the strains of Iraq mean that dealing with another major contingency would take more time and cost more in terms of casualties than would otherwise be the case.

Equally, the jewel in the crown of the special relationship has always been and remains the intelligence link. And yet, in the wake of the fallout from Iraq and the debacle over the weapons of mass destruction (WMD) issue, that link is surely the most tarnished element of all, at least for now. Intelligence is an area where, it is to be hoped, both countries are genuinely looking to learn lessons from the recent past, and have been re-evaluating the quality of the product they have been receiving recently, how it is used, and what it all means for their liaison.

Of course, the response always is that the intelligence successes inevitably must remain secret. But the recent presidential commission on U.S. intelligence capabilities regarding WMD concluded with respect to Iraq that "the harm done to American credibility by our all too public intelligence failings . . . will take years to undo."[2] The same presidential commission concluded that the United States still knows "disturbingly little" about the weapons programs and even less about the intentions of many of its most dangerous adversaries — which, by implication, include both Iran and North Korea. Such a situation clearly has considerable policy implications.[3]

It may take years for the intelligence communities in America and Britain to regain their morale — condemned as they seem to be to years of perpetual radical "reforms" — and to restore their credibility with elements of the policymaking establishments in both countries. On the other hand, it is clear that they need to change, having not adapted sufficiently to what is admittedly a more challenging security environment, and having been notoriously resistant in the past to external pressures for reform. In any event, it seems inevitable that the revelations they offer will be viewed in a rather different light in the future from the way they were previously.

It has often been remarked that the bar of proof that the United States will have to clear in the arena of international public opinion for any future intervention will be even higher now as a result of the experience of Iraq, making the construction of any future coalitions for action, willing or grudging, even more problematic. The question has also been raised as to whether a British prime minister, even the current one, could ever again sign up to a U.S.-led adventure like Iraq and take Britain to war in any similar circumstances. But the question is surely moot, since it must be equally inconceivable that any American president, even this American president, would be able to take HIS country to war again in the same set of circumstances as those of Iraq. Still, it must have raised a few eyebrows that the first published response by the new U.S. Secretary of State, Condoleezza Rice, to the presidential commission's conclusions on intelligence was that "there are no guarantees where intelligence is concerned," and that "while we may never know the exact nature of any of these [clandestine weapons] programs, we also have to be very careful not to underreact" to closed societies seeking WMD.

If the military and intelligence pillars of the special relationship are circumscribed for the time being, what of the broader foreign policy front? The great good fortune for this relationship has been that, in the mainstream struggle of the Cold War, the two countries were the founding fathers of the Western alliance and shared a common ideal. The good fortune for Britain in the post-Cold War world has been that the main cockpits of concern have been in regions where it retains both real and direct influence and interest—in Europe itself, notably the Balkans, and in the Middle East, notably Iraq.

More generally on the world stage, Washington and London have been far less in step. In the early post-World War II world, President Dwight Eisenhower's cool attitude to empire and colonialism was as problematic for Britain as it was for France, culminating for both imperial powers in the fiasco of Suez. But it felt so much more hurtful for London than for Paris. In the 1960s and 1970s there were the strains over Vietnam. Even the golden age of the Reagan-Thatcher years had their moments of crisis. In the prime minister's darkest hour, the Falklands crisis, Washington equivocated because the State Department feared what open support for Britain would do to U.S. interests in South America. The other oft-cited humiliation for London was the 1983 U.S. invasion of the Commonwealth country of Grenada. But the slight that surely must have been for Margaret Thatcher potentially the much more far-reaching was Ronald Reagan's summit with Mikhail Gorbachov in the Icelandic capital, Reykjavik, in October 1986, when the two men came close to a sweeping nuclear disarmament pact without so much as a passing thought for the British Prime Minister.

In the post-Reagan era, the ultimate diplomatist President, George H. W. Bush, gave Whitehall great cause for concern. His calculation of U.S. national interest and the likely international agenda prompted him early in his presidency to favor Germany over Britain. That sent shockwaves down the corridors of power in London. But more sober voices urged patience, counselled caution, and predicted that, when the chips were really down, the Americans would remember who their most trusted and valuable friends were.

So it proved to be. Vindication came in August 1990 when Iraq marched into Kuwait. The glue that kept the relationship solid over the next decade was none other than the former Iraqi president, Saddam Hussein. From the Kuwait invasion unfolded Operation DESERT STORM, the United Nations Special Commission (UNSCOM), the no-fly zones, containment (and the erosion of it), and finally—in the aftermath of September 11, 2001 (9/11)—Operation IRAQI FREEDOM. Now, of course, Iraq has morphed into the anvil on which the relationship has been most battered.

Without Iraq, things begin to look shaky on the foreign policy front. On some of the Bush administration's key agenda items, like North Korea, Taiwan, and the rise of China, Britain may have a view but hardly any influence. On those issues, Washington's key partners and friends will surely be Seoul, Tokyo, and perhaps even Delhi. Equally, Tony Blair may be the most Atlanticist prime minister imaginable, but, absent Iraq, he espouses a liberal and moral international agenda on poverty, debt relief, and climate change that hardly sets the Bush White House on fire.

So what is the diplomatic way forward for Britain in this unusual state of affairs? Tony Blair is clearly in the twilight of his premiership. His reduced parliamentary majority, and the fact that the locus of power is edging towards his assumed successor, Gordon Brown, give him less room for maneuver. Moreover, he has the image of "damaged goods" over Iraq, even if the charges that he was simply George Bush's "poodle" are wide of the mark.

Part of the Prime Minister's calculation over Iraq, for sure, was a desire to preserve the relationship and to be seen to be at America's side in its hour of greatest need. But Tony Blair was not a reluctant follower in the argument of the threat of proliferation and WMD. His public statements in the immediate aftermath of 9/11 were in some ways in advance of those emerging from Washington at the time. He also went further in publicly broaching a moral case for removing Saddam Hussein than did the Bush administration. And, with hindsight, he probably wishes he had pressed that case further still.

Equally, the concessions he extracted from Washington—in shaping its response to 9/11, on the U.S. *demarche* to the United Nations (UN) over Iraq, and over Middle East diplomacy—are not to be dismissed, especially given how otherwise deaf and impervious to the arguments of outsiders this particular U.S. administration generally is.

Part of the problem for Britain's international standing is its guilt by association with a vilified United States—so different from the times when everyone envied the closeness of the Thatcher-Reagan partnership, for example. Sorting out the temporary from the lasting elements of all that will be no small task.

On the other hand, events may be conspiring to offer some new hope. Events in Iraq shattered the Blair vision—not a new or original vision, but clearly passionately felt—of Britain as the indispensable bridge between the United States and Europe. British attitudes toward Europe are part of its enduring, post-imperial identity crisis. But, ironically, there may now be a window of opportunity to rebuild that concept, and the possibility that Britain can exert real influence in Washington even when the two do not see eye-to-eye through the vehicle of the European Union (EU).

Tony Blair may now look relatively weak domestically, but in comparison to most of his European counterparts, he is in a position of enviable strength. And, while the rows over the EU constitutional treaty and the budget may have provoked some serious political enmity between Britain and other key EU member states, they also offer the opportunity for Britain to press a reform agenda that would create a stronger but flexible Europe in which the British worldview could still hold sway. Above all, the EU also does not want to be seen as hobbled by internal debate, and it is more anxious than ever to be seen as an effective and constructive player on the world stage.

The happy coincidence is that America's and the EU's travails have also prompted even the most Euro-sceptical in the Bush administration to take a more benevolent view across the Atlantic. The EU constitutional debacle probably has banished the neo-con specter of a monolithic strategic rival. At the same time, the prospect of Europe retreating into a period of introspective soul-searching is actually sounding alarm bells in the administration at a time when its own traditional instruments of global power projection are hugely circumscribed by Iraq. It would clearly be beneficial to engage with partners like the EU. All these considerations produced perhaps the most harmonious atmosphere in years for a U.S.-EU meeting in Washington in the wake of the catastrophic EU summit in Brussels in June.

But if there is to be transatlantic engagement on British terms, it must also guide the agenda toward areas where it and Europe have common interests and real influence with Washington. That might be difficult, given how much Tony Blair has invested in his agenda for the economic development of Africa. But the issues are obvious: Iran, of course, for the time being at least; weapons proliferation in general; democratic prospects in Russia; and the challenge of an emerging China.

Apart from the EU pillar, the North Atlantic Treaty Organization (NATO) pillar also cannot be neglected. Britain must more actively press for further reform in the Atlantic Alliance. NATO is to a remarkable extent pursuing a Pentagon/Rumsfeld agenda in terms of modernizing its military capabilities, but it is doing so reluctantly and half-heartedly, especially in terms of how much Europe's NATO members are prepared to devote to defense spending. Moreover, there has hardly been the beginning of a debate on how NATO can organize itself for the future in order to use what capabilities it has. Nor has there been much substantive discussion about *when* to use these capabilities. Answers to these questions will determine NATO's continuing relevance. The technicalities of military capabilities are important, but more important is creating a new concept of operations for the Alliance.

Obviously, Britain itself cannot rest on its laurels as far as its own military capabilities are concerned. The current government has received many plaudits for the way it has transformed the British military through its initial Strategic Defence Review; and in technological and training terms, nobody is closer to the Americans than the British. But, as it pursues networked technology and transformational capabilities, Britain is perilously close to dipping below that critical mass of deployable force that would allow it to exercise real influence in the planning and execution of future interventionist missions on the scale of Iraq. Whatever government is in power in the coming years, it will have to look seriously and closely at what level of investment it is prepared to maintain in support of the country's armed forces. Still, the military and NATO contexts only can be one element of a much broader diplomatic picture. "Strategic lift" and "precision-guided munitions" will not be ultimate benchmarks of whether this partnership will endure.

And while America and Europe may have different ways of doing things, different traditions, and different strengths — in a fluid world in which powers of huge potential like India and China are on the rise — diplomatic engagement in an objective view must look more profitable than hostile for both America and Europe. This is so, regardless of America's current position as the world's only superpower and regardless of the European bloc's status as America's biggest trading partner. Instinctively, both sides of the Atlantic divide must also realize it surely cannot be in the interests of either America or Europe — let alone Britain — for the "ugly Americans" to be forever portrayed as wielding the big stick, while the "shifty Europeans" are always seen as tacking and maneuvering, managing and bargaining for everything but resolving nothing.

Yet the legacy of the last few years of ill will and suspicion is not to be underestimated. The efforts to bridge this divide cannot be helped by the fact that the domestic political standings of key actors on each side of the Atlantic look relatively weak at the moment.

Europe and Britain must also be wary of the fact that there is a debate within the right itself in Washington, not just between right and left, over what is the proper tone and course for U.S. foreign policy. For that reason, the jury must still be out as to the real motivation of Washington in terms of its European overtures.

The second Bush term has certainly been focused very closely on Europe so far. And Europeans can take some satisfaction from the number of times President Bush and his top aides actually have crossed the Atlantic to talk to them. The words emerging from American lips for the most part have been soothing ones. But the Europeans should not be complacent. It is not a foregone conclusion that this administration will remain engaged across the Atlantic indefinitely if it does not see positive results. There are probably still some voices with influence on the White House arguing that Europe should not be the center of its attention, that it is by no means the indispensable partner on many of the issues which exercise Washington at the moment, like North Korea or China. So it will be working through Europe that Britain has the best chance of maintaining the special relationship and ensuring it is a real one, with real give and take, and real dividends for both sides.

ENDNOTES - CHAPTER 9

1. Robert Woodward, *Plan of Attack*, New York: Simon & Schuster, 2004, pp. 237-238.

2. The Commission on the Intelligence Capabilities of the United States Regarding Weapons of Mass Destruction, March 31, 2005, p. 37.

3. *Ibid.*, Covering letter from the Commission.

CHAPTER 10

THE SPECIAL RELATIONSHIP AND FOREIGN POLICY: PANEL CHAIRMAN'S REPORT

Philip Stephens

What follows is the chairman's report of the conference panel sessions on foreign policy. Needless to say, it borrows heavily from the excellent contributions of the panel speakers, John Hulsman and Nicholas Childs, and from the dialogue in our sessions in Carlisle, Washington, Shrivenham, and London. But, as with any synthesis, its conclusions will obviously be partial and, to the degree that they exclude some points and add others, the responsibility for errors and omission lies fully with the chairman.

Our conference could not have been more timely. Events since the terrorist attacks of September 11, 2001 (9/11), including the war in Iraq, have exposed the enduring strengths of the special relationship. Rarely have a U.S. president and a United Kingdom (UK) prime minister worked so closely in pursuit of common foreign policy objectives as George W. Bush and Tony Blair. The interlocking strands of the relationship — historical, cultural, and economic as well as those in the traditional security arenas of defense and intelligence-sharing — are mutually reinforcing. The habit of cooperation is deeply ingrained.

Yet even at this moment of maximum cooperation, our proceedings recognized that the context for the relationship has changed fundamentally. The transatlantic alliance has lost the glue provided by a common enemy in the form of the Soviet Union; a much expanded European Union (EU) has fractured over Iraq; and a cultural chasm between conservative, religious America, and liberal, secular Europe has raised deeper questions about shared values. Britain's foreign policy establishment knows East Coast America; the Midwest and South are unfamiliar territory. The North Atlantic Treaty Organization (NATO), the vital hub of the postwar security alliance, has failed fully to adapt to the new global environment. The big conclusion that policymakers in Washington and London should draw from these changes is that theirs is no longer a friendship that can be taken for granted, but rather a relationship that must be worked at. Few could imagine divorce, but some of our number worried that, over time, this could become a marriage of separate lives.

The value for the UK of intimate engagement with Washington is that, matched by its place in the EU, it allows the occupant of 10 Downing Street to lay claim to a role in international affairs that would otherwise be denied a middle-ranking power. Tony Blair set out this ambition in a speech in the autumn of 1999. He alluded to Dean Acheson's famous remark some 40 years earlier that Britain had lost an empire and failed to find a role. This had indeed been the case, Blair said. But the world had moved on: "We have a new role ... not as a superpower but as a pivotal power, as a power that is at the crux of the alliances and international politics which shape the world and its future."[1] Blair's foreign policy has thus been guided by the hope, only sometimes fulfilled, that Britain can combine its position as America's closest friend with one of foreign policy leadership in the EU.

For the United States, the benefit lies in a reliable ally — a nation that, by and large, shares America's instincts and values and one, by virtue of history and tradition, that is willing to stand alongside Washington in moments of difficulty and conflict. During the Cold War, this translated into solidarity in the face of the Soviet threat. More recently, it has been reflected in Britain's decision to stand shoulder to shoulder with the United States in Afghanistan and Iraq. Even a sole superpower needs friends.

If most of the participants in our symposiums were optimistic that the partnership would endure, there was agreement that nothing should be taken for granted in a world as uncertain as the present one. During the 15 years since the collapse of the Soviet Union and the 4 years since the second geopolitical earthquake represented by 9/11, most, if not all, of the postwar arrangements established by Franklin D. Roosevelt, Harry S Truman, and Winston Churchill have come under scrutiny and strain. The world in 2005 is a different place from that of 1945, and the tectonic plates are still moving. After the fall of the Berlin Wall, the distinguished American political scientist, Francis Fukuyama, wrote a book characterizing the defeat of communism as the end of history.[2] It was a beguiling thesis, but premature. Surveying today's still-shifting geopolitical landscape, the same author might agree that the beginning of history would have been a more apposite choice.

If the post-World War II alliances and institutions are to endure, they will have to prove themselves again and, in most cases, be reshaped to meet the challenges of the 21st century. For the moment, the United States is the world's sole superpower, the "hyperpuissance" in the description of former French Foreign Minister Hubert Vedrine. The "status quo" power of the Cold War has since 9/11 become a revolutionary one, determined at once to intervene preemptively against its enemies and to embark on a long-term project to spread freedom and democracy in the Middle East. The United States is invincible but not invulnerable. The global order is being reshaped to reflect these new realities. The special relationship is no exception. Policymakers on both sides of the Atlantic recognize the worth of this particular alliance, but they have begun to appreciate that they must demonstrate its continuing relevance.

The two nations share the same global outlook. Tony Blair understood more clearly than most world leaders how profoundly the terrorist attacks on New York and Washington of 9/11 had changed forever the psychology of an America that has preferred to eschew foreign adventures. That appreciation and a parallel determination to stand alongside the United States, both reinforced by the bombings in London itself in July 2005, explain the warmth between London and Washington of recent years. Though Blair and Bush come from different places on the political spectrum, they have forged a strong personal relationship built on mutual trust. Blair is a frequent visitor to the White House and the two men speak regularly—often weekly—via a video link installed in the basement of 10 Downing Street.

Threat perceptions—from Islamist terrorism, proliferation of weapons of mass destruction (WMD), rogue and failing states—and assessments of the appropriate long-term responses, including encouragement for the spread of democracy in the Middle East, are also similar. After a period in which the White House seemed indifferent to Tony Blair's constant calls for action to resolve the

Palestinian-Israeli conflict, George W. Bush has adopted a policy of active engagement in the region. The transatlantic, and trans-European, wounds opened by the Iraq war—encapsulated in Secretary of Defense Donald Rumsfeld's sardonic characterization of the continent's division between Old and New Europe—have begun to close.

The participants in our conferences, though, also recognized the challenges to the relationship that have flowed from sometimes different approaches to the fight against terrorism, from the strategic implications of rising powers in Asia, and from a diverging approach to international institutions and law. Blair's aim has been to keep the United States committed to a vibrant transatlantic partnership, to a rules-based international system, and to global cooperation. The Bush administration often has been reluctant to accept such perceived constraints on its national sovereignty.

We should not idealize the special relationship. It is as much a product of national interests as of cultural affinities and historical affections. British prime minister Harold Macmillan once mused that the UK could act as Greece to America's Rome, steering "new world" power with "old world" wisdom. This conceit, though, has through the years both exaggerated British influence and underestimated American self-interest. Both partners have shown they can be hard-headed when national and mutual interests have seemed to diverge. In a masterful review of the historical roots of the alliance's foreign policy dimensions, Nicholas Childs reminded us of the many moments when opinions and interests have collided, straining our transatlantic ties. Dwight D. Eisenhower's disdain of empire forced Britain's humiliation at Suez in 1956. During the following decade, British prime ministers adamantly resisted pressure from Washington to commit their troops to the war in Vietnam. Margaret Thatcher danced on the world stage with Ronald Reagan in a close embrace, but there were sometimes fierce arguments when the music stopped. France, not the United States, proved Britain's most stalwart ally during the Falklands war. Washington provided vital intelligence and communications for the British task force in the South Atlantic, but only after a period of equivocation which saw Thatcher speak to her friend in the White House in the plainest possible terms. Reagan's flirtation with a sweeping nuclear disarmament pact with the Soviet

Union's Mikhail Gorbachev at the Rejkjavik summit ignored British interests. A few years later, George W. H. Bush deeply offended his closest ally by declaring a reunified Germany his most important strategic partner in Europe.

One could add to Nicholas Child's list the casual disregard for Britain's nuclear deterrent shown by John F. Kennedy when he cancelled the *Skybolt* missile system, and the deep divisions between John Major's government and the Clinton administration over the Balkans during the early 1990s. For some in Washington — including some in the present administration — the presumption that it should consult London often has seemed an unwelcome encumbrance.

During the post-World War II decades, the relationship weathered such storms — whatever their intensity, they were peripheral to the binding imperative to preserve the coherence of the Western alliance in the face of the Soviet threat — but they were a reminder that it is an essentially lop-sided partnership. One of the recurring themes of our conferences was a feeling that the British, with customary self-deprecation, have often underestimated their influence in Washington. That may be so. But while the occupant of 10 Downing Street can claim influence in Washington, the lesson of recent history is that power lies with his or her counterpart in the White House.

That said, our American participants stressed the importance of the alliance to Washington. John Hulsman set the special relationship in the broader transatlantic framework. The shifting sands of geopolitics meant that ties with London had to change, but that did not diminish their importance to the United States. The ingrained affinity between the two nations was a product of both common cultural heritage and a remarkably similar worldview. Britain was also one of only two European powers (the other is France) with the military capability and political will to project power in the world. In Hulsman's view, that made the UK a vital partner in the pursuit of America's global goals.

We caught a glimpse of this during the Iraq war. In the weeks before the toppling of the Baghdad regime, Secretary Rumsfeld stated publicly that the invasion would go ahead with or without the UK's armed forces.[3] The Defense Secretary's wholly undiplomatic remark spoke to the military reality: Britain's contribution in men and materiel to the removal of Saddam Hussein was significant but not vital. Yet the presence of British troops in the invasion force spoke to a political commitment of far greater significance—the more so as the security situation in Iraq deteriorated in the aftermath of the war.

In this part of our discussion, there was a discernible difference between some of our British and American participants. Childs, like Hulsman, set the relationship in the familiar context of a wider transatlantic alliance, but emphasized, from a British perspective, its interaction with the UK's European alliances. A unique friendship with Washington has served as one axis of a triangle which has also seen the UK seek to maximize its influence in an integrating EU. For most (not all) postwar British governments, the two sets of relationships have been seen as mutually reinforcing. Influence in Washington has been parlayed into a louder voice in Paris or Berlin, and vice versa. Such a balancing act, however, has rested on the assumption of U.S. support for closer European cooperation. That assumption has now been challenged as a consequence of German and French opposition to the Iraq war. Some in Washington—and John Hulsman put the case eloquently—believe that the United States should withdraw its support for European integration. In particular, it should see the development of a common European defense and security policy as a threat to NATO. Instead, in his view, the administration should focus on building up its bilateral relationships with like-minded European allies—the UK most certainly, but also newly democratized nations in the east such as Poland and the Baltic states. There are many in Washington who favor such a strategy of building coalitions of the willing instead of seeking accord with a cohesive EU. But the implications for a British government of such a policy would be serious: It would be forced to make the choice that, since Suez, it has done its utmost to avoid—as between the United States and Europe.

Such discussions invited the conclusion that policymakers face three sets of challenges in sustaining and adapting the special relationship. The first task was to recognize the potential strains, as well as the enduring strengths, in the relationship. Events since the terror attacks on New York and Washington on 9/11 have exposed a clash of strategic cultures between a United States determined to act decisively against its enemies and a Europe more wedded to the projection of "soft power" than of military might. Britain finds itself torn between the two: willing to act when necessary, but anxious that intervention carry international legitimacy.

Tony Blair has paid a significant political price for his staunch support of the Iraq war. The conventional wisdom has it that Blair joined the mission against Saddam Hussein in order to protect a privileged position in Washington. That is far too simplistic a view. The desire to preserve the strategic alliance certainly played a part in the dispatch of British troops to the Gulf. But Blair was as convinced as was George W. Bush that the Iraqi leader could not be permitted any longer to defy the international community. He agreed that the attacks of 9/11 had changed the nature of the threat posed by Saddam. Where others saw British obsequiousness to Washington, Blair saw a common foreign policy interest in upholding the will of the international community and in sending a powerful signal to those other nations that might be seeking to develop WMD.

These judgments were questioned, though, by the British electorate and by many in Blair's own Labour party. A widespread view in the UK has been that Bush and Blair misled their voters into war—a suspicion reinforced by the failure to uncover WMD in Iraq and by the rising cost in lives and treasure of the post-invasion insurgency. In spite of his third election victory in May 2005, Blair has paid dearly in terms of trust and popularity for the war. One consequence is that it would be difficult, if not impossible, for the prime minister, or indeed his eventual successor, to join the United States in a similar preemptive strike against potential enemies. If Bush had to struggle to secure congressional backing for such action, the occupant of 10 Downing Street would almost certainly fail to win the support of the House of Commons. More worryingly, the war and its bloody aftermath have nurtured a growing anti-Americanism among some sections of the British electorate. Events at Abu Ghraib prison in Iraq and the controversy over the rights of those held at Guantanamo Bay have led to questions in the UK about the extent to which values are still shared across the Atlantic.

Second, although Bush and Blair agreed to act in the face of hesitation at the United Nations (UN), there remains an underlying divergence in attitudes toward multilateral institutions and international law. Britain's instinct is that of most of its European neighbors, that threats to the global order are best met by responses that carry the stamp of international law and assent. It was Blair who prodded the President into seeking Resolution 1441 in the UN Security Council, and he desperately wanted a second resolution. Britain is part of the International Criminal Court, has signed up to the Kyoto treaty on climate change, and has supported the additional protocol for the chemical weapons convention. More recently, Blair's government has joined with those of France and Germany in seeking a negotiated end to Iran's uranium enrichment process. The present U.S. administration has made it clear that it supports multilateralism on sufferance. Most international agreements are seen as unacceptable constraints on its national sovereignty. The differences between Washington and London have thus far been bridgeable. It may not always be so.

Third, the geopolitical context for the special relationship has changed. For Britain, the close alliance with Washington was as much a product of the Anglo-French debacle at Suez in 1956 as the warmth of the wartime alliance between Churchill and Roosevelt. The ignominious withdrawal from Suez at Eisenhower's insistence marked the moment when the UK finally acknowledged that the sun had set on its great power status. As the retreat from empire accelerated, Harold Macmillan, who succeeded the discredited Anthony Eden, accepted that henceforth Britain could not engage in foreign adventures against the wishes of the United States. It was Macmillan who made the special relationship the *leitmotif* of British foreign policy for succeeding decades, combining it with the policy of active engagement with the leading powers of Europe. Blair's strategic vision of the UK as the pivotal power, or a bridge, between Europe and the United States was born of Macmillan's decisions.

The collapse of communism, however, has removed the overarching framework provided by the Soviet threat. Europe is no longer at the center of Washington's geopolitical interests — American security interests are linked more closely now to developments in the Middle East and Asia. Equally, in the absence of Soviet troop concentrations on the German borders, the U.S. security guarantee is no longer the *sine qua non* of European security. The weakening of

NATO as the essential forum for western security and the divisions within Europe over the Iraq war reflected these new geopolitical realities. They raise questions also over the durability of the UK's balancing act between the United States and Europe. For the past 40 years, it has avoided choosing between its American and European friends. Can it continue to do so?

The answer is "Yes, but." The strategic interests of Europe and the United States, and thus London and Washington, remain the same: Stability and freedom in the Middle East, a sustained path to democracy in Russia, partnership rather than rivalry with emerging great powers such as China and India, a global effort to separate moderate Islam from al Qaeda terrorism, and an effective brake on the profileration of unconventional weapons.

Mutual interests, however, are not a guarantee of mutual understanding. For 50 years the special relationship existed within the interlocking network of global institutions and treaties created after 1945. Many of these have been pushed to one side. The status quo superpower of the Cold War has become a hyperpower determined to remake the geopolitics of the Middle East and beyond. The United States looks out on a Hobbesian world in which overwhelming force is the most effective instrument of security; Britain views a terrain which also demands multilateral order and rules to avoid conflicts. Britain will strive to keep the special relationship, not only because it offers vital emotional reassurance for a power which still hankers after the influence of empire, but also because it depends on the United States for its nuclear deterrent. The special relationship also allows British prime ministers to take their place at the front of the international stage. But Europe is no longer America's front line. Will Washington continue to think it worth the indulgence?

ENDNOTES - CHAPTER 10

1. "Shaping a Pivotal Role For Britain in the World," Prime Minister's speech, Lord Mayor's Banquet, November 22, 1999, available at *www.fco.gov.uk/files/kfile/appendixjk.pdf*.

2. Francis Fukuyama, *The End of History and the Last Man*, New York: Free Press, 1992.

3. "Rumsfeld's Latest Ad-lib Riles Britain," *Chicago Tribune*, March 13, 2003, available at *www.chicagotribune.com/news/nationworld*.

SECTION IV:

SECURITY AND DEFENSE ASPECTS
OF THE SPECIAL RELATIONSHIP

CHAPTER 11

OBSERVATIONS ON THE SPECIAL RELATIONSHIP IN SECURITY AND DEFENSE MATTERS

Leo Michel

The substance of the U.S.-UK special relationship in security and defense matters was hardly mentioned during the 2005 parliamentary election campaign. British commentators agree, however, that broad public discomfort with Prime Minister Tony Blair's decision to cooperate closely with President George W. Bush on Iraq was a key factor in Labour's significant losses in the House of Commons. While it remains unclear how the voter's message and the reduction of Labour's majority in Westminster will affect specific outcomes on defense issues confronting the new Blair government (and its new Secretary of State for Defence, Dr. John Reid), it is reasonable to assume that Her Majesty's Government's (HMG) margin of maneuver on three fronts — the level of cooperation with U.S. forces in ongoing or possible future military operations; implementation of recent initiatives to restructure UK non-nuclear forces and capabilities (e.g., former Secretary of State for Defence Geoffrey Hoon's July 2004 Ministry of Defence report, *Delivering Security in a Changing World*); and looming future issues pertaining to the UK nuclear deterrent and role in missile defense — will be reduced. Ironically, these developments coincide with a marked increase in explicit and implied U.S. interest in broader and deeper security and defense cooperation with allies and partners, especially those — headed by the UK — with proven capabilities and a demonstrated political will to use them.

I intend, therefore, to focus on four areas:

- Impact of ongoing U.S. reviews affecting our defense strategy, military capabilities, and global and domestic basing posture;
- Future of nuclear cooperation;
- Missile defense; and,
- UK's "bridging" role between the United States and EU.

In addition, where possible, I will weave in some modest recommendations on what might be explored to maintain and strengthen the special relationship that has largely benefited both our nations.

Defense Strategy.

The U.S. Department of Defense (DoD) is engaged in a number of high-level assessments and planning efforts that will reshape American strategy and capabilities for years, if not decades, to come. These include the:

- *National Defense Strategy* and *National Military Strategy* (developed in parallel and released in early 2005);
- *2005 Quadrennial Defense Review* (now underway and due to Congress in February 2006);
- *Global Posture Review* (now in the negotiation and implementation stage); and,
- *Base Realignment and Closure* recommendations approved by the Congress and President in November 2005.

Taken individually, none of these efforts represents a radical departure from core concepts developed during the first year or two of the Bush administration. Together, however, they probably represent a watershed in its efforts to "transform" American defense and its relationship with allies. Having analyzed "lessons learned" during the post-Cold War period and the aftermath of September 11, 2001 (9/11) — and, in particular, its heavy engagement in Iraq and Afghanistan — the defense establishment and, in time, the White House and Congress will need to make a series of tough decisions on U.S. strategic priorities and resource allocations; the size, structure, equipment, and basing posture of U.S. military forces; and, of course, American relations with allies and partners.

To describe these processes as "complex" would be grossly inadequate (even by British standards of understatement). Moreover, they do not necessarily predict how the United States might act in any specific crisis. But understanding how American strategists assess the evolving international security environment, as well as the forces and capabilities needed to protect and advance American interests, provides a good a set of clues to future American actions. This, in turn, might be of some help in determining how the UK—alone, or with the United States, or in cooperation with other nations—should frame its strategy and configure its military forces and capabilities.

By way of background, here is a thumbnail sketch of the key reports. In the *National Defense Strategy*, the Secretary of Defense provides guidance to DoD on what it must do to implement the President's *National Security Strategy* of September 2002.[1] (The latter is still in force and covers the broad range of national security concerns and tools, not just those under Defense's purview.) A few points deserve emphasis:

- First, the *National Defense Strategy*'s opening sentence— "America is a nation at war"—speaks volumes. "Today's war," the report continues later, "is against terrorist extremist networks, including their state and non-state supporters." Although the term "Global War On Terrorism" rankles many in Europe, who might see it as either simplistic or dangerous or both, terrorism is the most acute manifestation of what the document calls "irregular challenges," i.e., challenges coming from those using unconventional means to counter traditional advantages of stronger opponents. However, "irregular challenges" are not the only category of strategic threat facing the United States. The document also identifies "traditional challenges" posed by states employing recognized military capabilities and forces; "catastrophic challenges" involving the acquisition, possession, and use of weapons of mass destruction (WMD); and "disruptive challenges" from adversaries seeking break-through technologies to counter current U.S. advantages in key operational domains. Moreover, these challenges might overlap; for example, al Qaeda is an "irregular" threat but is actively seeking "catastrophic" capabilities. Indeed, one reasonably could argue that, if evaluated in terms of likelihood and U.S. vulnerabilities, the potential combination of "irregular" and "catastrophic" challenges is the most pressing security problem facing us. That said, we do not have the luxury of focusing on only one or two challenges; thus, the strategy addresses the need to fight today's fight, while simultaneously reassuring allies and friends and preparing to dissuade, deter, or defeat future adversaries in an environment of "strategic uncertainty."

- Second, against this backdrop, the *National Defense Strategy* notes that U.S. forces currently are shaped and sized, at least in principle, to meet four major objectives set by the 2001 *Quadrennial Defense Review*: (1) to defend the U.S. homeland; (2) to assure allies and friends through forward deterrence in four critical regions; (3) to swiftly defeat adversaries in two overlapping military campaigns; and (4) to "win decisively" (this includes the so-called "regime change" option) in one of those campaigns. These objectives are to be met while preserving the U.S. ability to conduct a limited number of "lesser contingencies." In Pentagon jargon, this is known as the "1-4-2-1 planning construct."

- Third, the strategy emphasizes that "battlefield success" is only one element of a long-term, multifaceted U.S. campaign against terrorism. Other military activities (such as training and assistance to humanitarian efforts) as well as nonmilitary efforts (such as diplomacy, strategic communications, law enforcement, and economic sanctions) also must be employed. As underscored several times in the report, this places a very high premium on strengthening alliances and partnerships with nations (in both military and nonmilitary spheres) that share our interests and principles — although, as noted in the report, "even among our closest partners, threats will be perceived differently and consensus may be difficult to achieve."

- Fourth, notwithstanding the multiple references to working with allies and partners to develop an "active, layered defense" and to prevent problems from becoming crises, the strategy states: "Allowing opponents to strike first — particularly in an era of proliferation — is unacceptable." The strategy refers to the President's range of options, including a single mention of "preempt(ing) a devastating attack," but contains a potentially sweeping statement of intent: "At the direction of the President, we will defeat adversaries at the time, place, and in the manner of our choosing — setting the conditions for future security."

In the *National Military Strategy*, the Chairman of the Joint Chiefs of Staff takes the broad guidance within the *National Security Strategy* and *National Defense Strategy* and translates this into a set of military objectives from which U.S. combatant commanders and the military services identify the capabilities they desire and against which the Chairman assesses risk.[2] Hence, the *National Military Strategy* emphasizes the changing nature of military challenges, including: a wider spectrum of adversaries, ranging from states to nonstate organizations and individuals; a more complex "battlespace," encompassing densely populated urban areas (as experienced in Iraq) as well as some of the most remote and inhospitable terrain (as in Afghanistan); and the global proliferation of technology and advanced weaponry that could "dramatically increase an adversary's ability to threaten" the United States.

To counter such challenges, the *National Military Strategy* lays out a series of steps necessary to apply the three key principles to be considered by combatant commanders in planning and conducting operations: "agility" (i.e., the ability to rapidly deploy, employ, sustain, and redeploy capabilities in geographically separated and diverse regions); "decisiveness" (i.e., the ability to overwhelm adversaries, control situations, and achieve definitive outcomes without necessarily large force deployments); and "integration" (i.e., ensuring military activities are synchronized across military services, other government agencies and nongovernment organizations, and with overseas allies and partners).

In some respects, the *National Defense Strategy* and *National Military Strategy* can be seen as the political and doctrinal foundation of the 2005 *Quadrennial Defense Review*, the congressionally mandated report that recommends the capabilities needed to execute strategy. In the 1997 and 2001 *Quadrennial Defense Review*, the defense strategy was an output of the reviews; this year, the *National Defense Strategy* was decided first. Specifically, the *Quadrennial Defense Review* will be looking at four "core problems":

- What capabilities are needed to build partnerships to defeat extremism?

- What capabilities are needed to defend the homeland in depth?

- What capabilities are needed to shape the choices of countries at a "strategic crossroads"?

- What capabilities are needed to prevent the acquisition or use of WMD by hostile state or nonstate actors?

Among the six high-level civilian and military panels preparing to execute the review, the three panels likely to produce the most visible changes in military posture will examine: (1) "capabilities mix" issues affecting force structure and modernization; (2) "manning and balancing" issues focusing on personnel; and (3) "enablers," i.e., the capabilities essential to transforming the military, including airlift, sealift, logistics, and command, control, communications, computers, intelligence, surveillance, and reconnaissance (C4ISR). One should not discount, however, the import of the panel examining "roles and missions," which will look *inter alia* at how DoD is organized, and how it interacts with other U.S. government agencies, to address the range of strategic challenges.

The review must tackle a number of tough questions, many of which will have significant consequences for how the United States apportions its defense budget, what risks it is willing to take, and what trades it might make among capabilities options to mitigate those risks. (According to senior defense officials, the review panels are told *not* to assume continuing real increases in defense spending. This leads some analysts to view the *Quadrennial Defense Review* as a critical tool to determine how much "transformation" must be trimmed to accommodate rising personnel costs. Of course, the potential trades between transformation and personnel costs are just one example among many others.) Examples of such potential questions might include:

- How best to reconfigure and equip ground forces to confront the stubborn, low-tech, but deadly insurgency-terrorist enemies of the Iraqi type? How will the acknowledged importance of certain capabilities required for such warfare—including information warfare, special forces, and civil-military affairs and military police units—fare in the inevitable competition over budgets?

- How best to reduce the ratio of administrative and support personnel to combat forces, and to reduce the strain on reserve forces? Regarding the latter, does the United States need a permanent increase in the size of its active duty land component (Army and/or Marines) and, if so, by how many, in what areas, and how fast?

- How best to integrate and scale down redundant and costly programs in areas such as missile defense and advanced combat aircraft? (Congressional resistance to recently proposed budget cuts affecting, for example, the F/A-22 "Raptor" fighter and C-130J Hercules transport plane illustrates the problem.)

- How should the United States construct its C4ISR capabilities in ways such that valued allies can "plug into" U.S. systems? More broadly, is the United States prepared to make tradeoffs in its capabilities in order to cooperate better with partners (European and non-European) who, in some areas, are not so capable—and, if so, where and at what levels of risk?

- What DoD capabilities are needed to support the Department of Homeland Security and state and local authorities in the event of new terrorist attacks inside the United States? In this regard, according to recent press reports, the *Quadrennial Defense Review* will look at what would be necessary to respond to a small number of simultaneous attacks involving mass casualties.

Completing this picture are the *Global Posture Review* and the *Base Realignment and Closure* process. Under the former, DoD is moving to implement the President's plan outlined in August 2004 (after a 3-year review and extensive consultation with allies) to update U.S. military presence overseas and leverage 21st century military technologies. The plan follows major redeployments and adjustments in U.S. force structure that have been underway since the early 1990s, as American defense strategy adjusted to the end of the Cold War. Over the next decade, this plan is expected to result in the return to the United States of some 70,000 uniformed personnel and 100,000 civilian employees and dependents.

Details of the plan are still under discussion with allies and partners around the world, but the basic architecture is fairly well set.

- In Europe, roughly two brigades of "heavy" forces designed for Cold War-type scenarios—forces that have spent much of the last decade operating outside the continent—will return to the United States. In Germany, for example, General James L. Jones, USMC (Combatant Commander for Europe) foresees reducing the number of major U.S. Army communities from 14 to 4 and redeploying about 37,000 of the existing 62,000 troops back to the United States by late 2010. Meanwhile, a U.S. *Stryker* Brigade Combat Team and enablers will be stationed at Grafenwoehr, Germany, by late 2007, with an additional rotational brigade combat team to operate out of relatively austere forward operating sites in Eastern Europe. Ground, air, and naval headquarters will be streamlined and consolidated. Special forces, both forward-stationed and rotational, will increase in importance.[3]

- In Northeast Asia, about 12,500 troops will be removed from the Republic of Korea during 2005-08. U.S. military headquarters will shift from Seoul to Osan, and U.S. forces close to the Demilitarized Zone will move in phases to locations south of the Han River, out of North Korean artillery range. Additional advanced air and naval strike assets will be stationed in the Western Pacific. Washington and Tokyo are discussing a possible realignment of U.S. forces in Japan, but major reductions below the 45,000 troops currently deployed appear unlikely. In Central and Southeast Asia, the United States is working to establish a network of austere sites to provide training opportunities and access both for conventional and special forces.

- In the Middle East, cooperation and access provided by coalition partners during Operations ENDURING FREEDOM and IRAQI FREEDOM provide a solid basis for other forms of future cooperation. Sites for rotational forces and contingency

154

purposes, supported by forward headquarters and advanced training facilities, are envisaged, subject to the approval of the sovereign governments in the region.

In all of these regions, it is important to focus on capabilities — not just numbers of forces. Thanks to decades of investment, U.S. armed forces have achieved enormous advances in speed, reach, precision, and combat power. The number of forward-based forces in a given area is not the best measure of the military capability that the United States can bring to bear. Those who have suggested that these reductions will necessarily do grave damage to the North Atlantic Treaty Organization (NATO) are mistaken. The United States will retain substantial combat power in Europe, along with a robust reinforcement capability to deal with unexpected contingencies. The U.S. Joint Forces and European Commands are working closely with NATO's Allied Command Transformation to ensure that allies and partners benefit from advanced training and experimentation in combined activities with U.S. forces.

The fifth round since 1988 of the *Base Realignment and Closure* process has resulted in the proposed closure of 33 major domestic U.S. military bases and the realignment of an additional 29. Some existing facilities might be expanded to accommodate troops brought home from overseas. As in the past, this effort has involved difficult political negotiations and potential tradeoffs involving operations, training, and readiness. Still, the potential long-term savings to the Pentagon could amount to billions of dollars annually — freeing resources that can be plowed into personnel, equipment, and operations.

Against this backdrop, one can identify two broad areas where these various U.S. assessments and plans might affect the special relationship.

Strategy — Implications for the UK.

There is substantial positive news for the UK, in my view, in the *National Defense Strategy* and *National Military Strategy*. The U.S. experiences in Iraq and Afghanistan, in particular, seem to have brought home the lesson that the United States needs stronger and broader international partnerships to meet its strategic objectives and to pursue an "active, layered defense" of its homeland and interests. As the *National Defense Strategy* puts it bluntly: "The U.S. cannot achieve its defense objectives alone." Moreover, the Pentagon leadership acknowledges with unaccustomed clarity that these partnerships must be nurtured across a cohesive set of activities. These range from working with others to develop a common appreciation of threats, to increasing the capabilities and leadership roles of others, in both military and nonmilitary spheres, to prevent and defeat "irregular" challenges. Indeed, the *National Defense Strategy*'s language that "we must confront challenges earlier and more comprehensively" seems to echo that of the UK's *New Chapter of the Strategic Defence Review* (2002) and EU's *European Security Strategy* (2003). In addition, the renewed emphasis on broad security cooperation is eerily reminiscent of the Clinton administration's "engagement and shaping" strategy that was not exactly embraced after the 2000 elections. More important, perhaps, is the implicit recognition that "made in the USA" threat assessments and strategies are not the best way to engage and sustain the international partnerships that the United States so manifestly needs.

In a slightly more speculative vein, the *National Defense Strategy's* acknowledgement that, in a more complex world, the United States might not always agree with even its closest allies could be viewed as a nod toward the special relationship. In other words, if differences with the UK are anticipated, they probably can be better managed without a divorce.

That said, certain concerns of UK news media commentators and political-military analysts over the past few years likely will not be allayed by the strategy documents. For example, UK officials and strategic reviews have shied away from references to the "Global War on Terrorism," although their perception of key threats to UK national security are essentially identical to Washington's: international terrorism, WMD proliferation, regional conflict, and failed (or failing) states. Moreover, with the deadly July 2005 terrorist attacks against London's mass transit system, UK public perceptions of the threat may move even closer to the U.S. view. However, despite the multiple (and patently deliberate) U.S. references to the key role of "allies and partners," neither strategy document specifically mentions

NATO as the primary vehicle for U.S. cooperation with its European allies on strategy or capabilities development. For those Britons who have grown uncomfortable with the perceived U.S. proclivity for "coalitions of the willing," this might be a troublesome omission. And while the UK certainly has never forsworn its willingness to act alone if it deems its vital interests to be at stake, the aforementioned statement of U.S. presidential prerogatives might strike some British opinion leaders as unnecessary and possibly unhelpful.

Capabilities—Implications for the UK.

The *2005 Quadrennial Defense Review* and *Global Posture Review* likely will have more visible and practical consequences for the special relationship. Taking the *Global Posture Review* first, based on General Jones' statement, the U.S. Air Force intends to maintain and, indeed, recapitalize critical base infrastructure at Lakenheath (the only U.S. F-15 fighter wing based in Europe) and Mildenhall, UK. At Mildenhall, U.S. air refueling, air mobility, reconnaissance, and intelligence units apparently will not be repositioned, but the special forces air component likely will be moved during the 2011-15 period as part of a planned consolidation of permanent and rotational special operations forces in Southern Europe.[4] (Although not covered by General Jones' statement, one would assume that U.S. access to base facilities in Diego Garcia will remain important for both countries.)

The UK enjoys a privileged position in the preparation of the *2005 Quadrennial Defense Review*, as British Defence Ministry experts are for the first time "embedded" in the Office of the Secretary of Defense staff that coordinates the review. This is a tangible sign that the promise of the *National Defense Strategy* to work closely with allies in strategy and capabilities development is being implemented.

The Institute for National Strategic Studies does not participate as such in the *2005 Quadrennial Defense Review,* and it would be premature to predict the review outcomes. However, it is possible to identify some of the issues that likely will be of particular interest to the UK as the review progresses.

First, one must consider our respective military levels of ambition. A senior Pentagon official recently indicated that the previously mentioned "1-4-2-1 planning construct," which was agreed to shortly before the 9/11 attacks, could change as a result of the review. Although this might seem like an arcane exercise, the planning assumptions that lie behind this construct, or its possible successor, will help determine where the U.S. military is prepared to trade some of its unparalleled capability in conventional warfare to improve capabilities against the other types of threats identified in the *National Defense Strategy* — that is, the "irregular," "catastrophic," and "disruptive" challenges.

The thrust of the July 2004 Ministry of Defence report, *Delivering Security in a Changing World*, is the UK's level of ambition to "support three concurrent small and medium scale operations," while retaining the "flexibility to reconfigure for less frequent large scale operations, while concurrently conducting a small scale operation."[5] The UK report further states: "The full spectrum of capabilities is not required for large scale operations, as the most demanding operations could only conceivably be undertaken alongside the U.S., either as a NATO operation or a U.S.-led coalition, where we have choices as to what to contribute." In such large-scale operations, the range of potential UK contributions would include special forces, C4ISR assets able to be integrated with the U.S. network, amphibious and carrier strike task groups, an air expeditionary task force, and a land maneuver division capable of conducting offensive operations.

What happens, however, if the U.S. "planning construct" were to change? Would this change the desired balance among UK capabilities? If the United States, for example, were to significantly enlarge its special operations forces (based on an assessment that "irregular challenges" have become more pressing than "traditional" ones), should the UK follow suit so that it can, to cite the Ministry's report once more, "add real weight to the campaign and hence the UK's ability to influence its outcome"?[6] Or should the UK instead shift its relative effort to one or more of its other areas of special strength, such as forces and capabilities useful for post-conflict stabilization? Would this translate into a requirement for a larger UK ground force (as some American experts are arguing is the case for the United States) or, at a minimum, not reducing its existing levels?

Second, assuming the planned size and mix of UK forces are settled, a key to effective cooperation with the United States in operations will be the ability to integrate respective C4ISR capabilities.

The *National Defense Strategy* and *National Military Strategy* place such great emphasis on these key operational capabilities that it is hard to imagine that the 2005 *Quadrennial Defense Review* and subsequent budgetary decisions will not follow suit. Recognizing that the Ministry's report also emphasizes the importance of C4ISR, we then must ask: will the UK be able to keep apace with U.S. efforts in this area? A host of financial and technological issues, to include sensitive issues of technology-sharing arrangements, are likely to flow from the review's recommendations.

Third, as the United States determines what capabilities are needed to shape the choices of countries arriving at strategic crossroads (China and Russia come to mind, although these have not been explicitly cited by American officials) or to prevent the acquisition of use of WMD by a hostile state or nonstate actor, what will be the UK's role? For the United States, missile defenses are one means of dissuading, deterring, and if necessary defending against a limited missile attack by a "rogue" nation. The twin strategy reports also seem to presage a wider use of small-scale military activities (for example, training and exercises) to build the capabilities of others. Will the UK be similarly inclined to increase its current contribution to such activities?

Fourth, as the Pentagon (and the U.S. government as a whole) looks at its capabilities and structures to deal with homeland security, what lessons can we learn from the UK's experience over the years? The need for close U.S.-UK cooperation in this area obviously transcends defense-to-defense channels, and — as we saw from 9/11, its aftermath, and now July 7, 2005 (7/7), in London — our common security, political, and economic stakes in this area are enormous.

Future of Nuclear Cooperation.

The *National Defense Strategy* and *National Military Strategy* barely mention the role of U.S. nuclear weapons. This is understandable for a few reasons: the changed relationship with Russia; the priority given to capabilities needed to confront the "irregular" threats from insurgencies and international terrorism; and, perhaps, a desire to avoid any perceived brandishing of nuclear capabilities at a time when the United States is relying heavily on diplomatic tools to resolve concerns with North Korean and Iranian nuclear developments.

An additional explanation might be that little of substance has changed since the *Nuclear Posture Review* was completed in late 2001. To briefly recap some of the main findings of this review:

- Reliance on nuclear weapons should be reduced by developing non-nuclear offensive and defensive capabilities that allow the United States to raise the nuclear threshold.

- In keeping with the President's guidance to reduce the number of operationally deployed nuclear weapons to the lowest possible level, and to do so without some of the drawbacks of Cold War-style arms control negotiations and treaties, the United States will look toward unilateral reductions. In terms of force sizing, the *Nuclear Posture Review* set a goal of 1,700-2,200 operationally deployed warheads by 2012 (which represents a reduction of approximately 3,800 warheads from the level permitted by START I, which remains in force).

- Given the existing and emerging threat to the United States and its allies and friends from WMD and missile proliferation, U.S. nuclear planning needs to become more capable against a range of contingencies and less country-specific. The President needs a "more diverse portfolio of capabilities" — to include nuclear forces, non-nuclear strike forces, and missile defenses — to assure allies and friends, and dissuade, deter, and, if necessary, defeat adversaries.

- So-called "life extension programs" would keep the current types of delivery systems in service until 2020 or longer. This represents an important budgetary and technical effort, as the average ages of U.S. delivery systems (when the review was completed) were 26 years for the *Minuteman III* intercontinental ballistic missile, 9 years for the *Trident II* D-5 submarine-launched ballistic missile, 40 years for the B-52 bomber, and 5 years for the B-2 bomber. Four of the 18 *Trident* strategic ballistic missile submarines (SSBNs) would be taken out of strategic service, and the remaining 14 SSBNs would be fitted with *Trident II* D-5 missiles. In addition, the *Peacekeeper* land-based intercontinental ballistic missiles (ICBMs) would be retired, and the B-1 bomber force would no longer be maintained for a nuclear weapon role.

- The United States would rely on its "stockpile stewardship" program designed to ensure the safety and reliability of the nuclear weapons stockpile without nuclear testing, but it would not ratify the Comprehensive Test Ban Treaty (CTBT). It also would study options to reduce the preparatory time needed — currently somewhere between 2 to 3 years — if the President were to determine that a resumption of nuclear testing was necessary to rectify a stockpile problem.[7]

The special relationship as related to nuclear weapon systems has had a long and enviable history. Indeed, there exists no other program where the United States has worked so intimately with another country for such an extended period of time on the gravest matters of national security. This aspect of our special relationship remains very much alive. One could posit that this relationship grows even more important as the size of our respective nuclear arsenals has shrunk over the past decade.

It perhaps is worth recalling that a relationship that many take for granted today has not always been problem-free. During World War II, Anglo-American cooperation on nuclear matters was not covered by any binding legal agreements, and postwar cooperation was virtually stopped by the *U.S. Atomic Energy Act of 1954.* That law was not amended until early 1958, clearing the way, in July of that year, for the *U.S.-UK Agreement on Cooperation on the Use of Atomic Energy for Mutual Defense Purposes.* The agreement authorizes a broad range of cooperation on information, training, material, and equipment, but bars any transfer of a nuclear weapon by either party. Less than 5 years later, however, the "Skybolt affair" came close to wrecking U.S.-UK nuclear cooperation for a second time. Fortunately, an extraordinary set of negotiations between President John Kennedy and Prime Minister Harold Macmillan in December 1962 — nearly 4 days of what Macmillan described in his memoirs as "fierce and sometimes painful (arguments)" — produced the "Nassau Agreement," which set the stage for formal arrangements for the U.S. sale of *Polaris* missiles for UK submarines and, subsequently, the sale of *Trident II* D-5 missiles and launch systems for the UK's Vanguard-class submarines.[8]

Accounts of the Nassau Agreement make for fascinating reading in light of subsequent developments. For example, Macmillan wrote that his government kept General Charles de Gaulle apprised of the Nassau talks on a day-to-day basis. He also hinted that he encouraged Kennedy's subsequent offer of *Polaris* missiles to the French on terms similar to those agreed for the UK. Another observation by Macmillan seems particularly relevant. "The Americans," he wrote, "were willing to defend Europe and had the means to do so. Would they always have the will? America must realize that the great nations of Europe, with their different histories and varying responsibilities, would demand a reasonable degree of dignity and security. Certainly Britain with her world-wide commitments must continue, for the present at any rate, to have some independent nuclear force."[9]

The international security environment obviously has changed since Macmillan's days. And unlike the days of the Skybolt affair, when some in the UK suspected the United States of wanting to "force Britain out of the nuclear club," Washington's decades-long record of strong support for an independent UK deterrent shows no signs of eroding.[10] Last year, the United States and UK agreed to a 10-year extension of their 1958 Agreement, and President Bush, in his letter to Congress on this subject, wrote that "the United Kingdom intends to continue to maintain viable nuclear forces." The question now seems to be whether the UK in the coming years will reach the same conclusion as Macmillan. Specifically, will the UK opt to maintain its SSBN capability through cooperation with the United States, or diversify its nuclear delivery capability (perhaps in cooperation with France), or choose to allow its minimal nuclear deterrent to atrophy?

Timing will no doubt play an important role here. In the case of the *Trident II* system, the United States has been able to extend the SSBN's service life from 30 to 45 years. To address the mismatch between SSBN's service life and the nominal 30-year service life of its D5 missile, the United States has begun a D5 "life extension" program (which includes the purchase of additional missiles as well as the replacement of some aging components) that will make it possible to retain the *Trident II* system until 2020 or longer. However, for a number of reasons, the UK likely will need to decide on a follow-on to its *Trident II* system during the next Parliament—that is, in advance of an eventual U.S. decision on its own *Trident II* follow-on.

I assume that the UK will want to keep a credible minimum nuclear deterrent for the foreseeable future, given the extant and potential future threats of WMD and missile proliferation. How the UK might define "credible" and "minimum" in the future are yet to be determined; as demonstrated by the *Strategic Defence Review* in 1998, UK assessments of its nuclear force requirements are subject to change over time. In any event, given the security, technological, industrial, and budgetary ramifications of such decisions, the importance of close and timely U.S.-UK consultations on their possible future cooperation would seem self-evident. Neither side can afford the type of missed signals and lack of forethought that characterized the Skybolt debacle.

This leads to three final observations. First, it seems to me that the U.S. decision not to pursue traditional Cold War-style nuclear arms agreements with Russia holds a significant benefit from a UK perspective: it effectively moots any future Russian attempt to limit the independent UK (and French) deterrent as a price for further negotiated reductions with the United States. Second, without discounting the importance, both real and potential, of increasing British defense cooperation with its European partners in conventional systems, it is hard for me at least to imagine alternative UK arrangements in the nuclear field—for example, either bilaterally with France or within a broader European context—that would match the strategic, technical, and cost benefits of its established relationship with the United States. Third, UK defense planners will need to consider some difficult budgetary trade-offs between future conventional and nuclear capabilities if, as most observers believe, significant real increases in the defense budget are not in the offing. Given the relatively recent "conversion" of New Labor to support for a "minimum" nuclear deterrent and the increased political sensitivities regarding close cooperation with the United States, a well-thought-out public campaign to explain HMG's nuclear policy will be absolutely critical to sustaining any decision regarding a *Trident II* follow-on.

Missile Defense.

As of late December 2004, the United States had emplaced six ground-based mid-course defense (GMD) interceptor missiles in underground silos at Fort Greely, Alaska, and one GMD interceptor at Vandenberg Air Force Base, California. If current plans hold, by the end of 2005 the United States will have deployed an additional 10 GMD interceptors at Fort Greely and a second interceptor at Vandenberg, along with land-, sea-, and space-based sensors and command and control systems to support those weapons and up to eight Standard Missile-3 sea-based interceptors. These initial deployments are only the first step on the path to the administration's goal of an integrated, global missile defense to protect the United States, its allies, and friends with deployed forces against limited attacks by ballistic missiles of all ranges and in all phases of flight. The main concern driving this goal is not the ballistic missile force of major powers such as Russia; rather, it is the proliferation of WMD and ballistic missile capabilities of states such as North Korea and Iran. Indeed, for the most part, the administration has been careful not to oversell the initial U.S. defensive capabilities, characterizing the first deployments as "very basic" and a "nascent defensive system."

To date, U.S.-UK cooperation related to missile defense has been limited but important. In February 2003, the UK gave the United States permission to upgrade the U.S.-owned, RAF-operated *Fylingdales* early warning radar, which is important to track potential threats from the Middle East region. Later that year, the sides signed a new memorandum of understanding on missile defense cooperation covering arrangements for joint work on system research, development, testing, and evaluation. These arrangements currently include British participation within DoD's Missile Defense Agency in Washington and Colorado Springs. In addition, reflecting the high level of U.S. transparency with regard to the UK on missile defense operational issues, British officers are "embedded" in the U.S. Strategic Command.

In addition to these bilateral arrangements, the United States and UK have worked within NATO to reach an Alliance consensus on a missile defense feasibility study, which was due to be completed by July 2005. That study examines the option of defending territory and population centers against the full range of missile threats. It also would complement Alliance agreement on an active layered Theater Missile Defense against short- and medium-range missile threats, wherein NATO would provide a command and control architecture that would be interoperable with sensors and interceptors fielded by individual nations.

The United States has not asked the UK to base GMD interceptors on its territory, and the UK has not decided to do so. That said, several of the operational issues facing senior U.S. decisionmakers, military commanders, and defense planners would need to be considered by the UK or other Allies that might be weighing such moves.[11] For example,

- Who would have weapons release authority? The timeline for decisions on launching interceptors is significantly shorter than the flight time for offensive ballistic missiles, which ranges from a few minutes for short-range systems to 20-30 minutes for missiles of intercontinental range. Given such short timelines, it would seem infeasible to insist on a specific prior authorization from the political leadership to launch a defensive weapon. More likely, such authorization would need to be delegated to an appropriate level of military authority.

- Assuming limited defensive assets, at least in the initial stages of deployment, what criteria should be employed in deciding which enemy missiles to target and how many interceptors should be allocated to them? Given the combination of possible intelligence uncertainties about the number of missiles available to the adversary and a defender's preference to put multiple interceptors against each threatening missile (to have a higher probability of a successful intercept), defenders might face tough choices. For example, would defenders place highest priority on maximizing the population saved, or protecting the ability of government to continue functioning, or protecting other essential military capabilities? And if it is unclear whether the target of the offensive missile (or missiles) is one's own territory or that of a neighbor, how should this be factored into a decision whether to launch interceptors and, if so, how many to launch?

- What would be the appropriate role for senior government decisionmakers on the employment of missile defenses? Under the stress of attack, when defenders would be calculating what interceptor assets they have left and how best to use them, there would be precious little time for second-guessing. Presumably, the government leadership would have promulgated guidance during peacetime planning, subject to review and revision in the buildup to a crisis. At a minimum, government decisionmakers would need accurate, real-time information about the ongoing missile defense engagements, in part to determine whether to authorize either nuclear or non-nuclear strikes against strategic targets. It should not be forgotten, in this context, that effective missile defenses would give the leadership greater latitude in choosing a response to the attack—perhaps one that does not threaten massive casualties on the part of the state from where the attack originated.

These are instances of the complex and vital questions associated with the deployment of missile defenses. While not unanswerable, they will require timely and serious attention as the UK considers its future level of cooperation with the United States in this area.

UK as a "Bridge" between the United States and EU.

Europeans can be forgiven for occasionally asking if Americans *really* support the EU's European Security and Defense Policy (ESDP). Since NATO's creation in 1949, Washington has alternately encouraged and hectored its allies to assume a larger share of the responsibilities and burdens of collective defense and—beginning with NATO's involvement in Bosnia in 1995—crisis response. At the same time, Republican and Democratic administrations alike have looked to NATO as the anchor of U.S. engagement in European security affairs and the primary multilateral venue for shaping allies' defense policies and capabilities.

Hence, when Prime Minister Blair and President Jacques Chirac agreed at St. Malo, France, in December 1998 that the EU "must have the capacity for autonomous action, backed up by credible military forces, the means to decide to use them and a readiness to do so, in order to respond to international crises," Washington's initial response was polite but distinctly chilly. Fresh memories of intra-European wrangling over the former Yugoslavia in the early 1990s, combined with growing worries about the situation in Kosovo, no doubt played a role here. Some Americans worried whether, to use then French Defense Minister Alain Richard's analogy, the EU would be capable of "taking care of fires in its own backyard." Or would the EU, to be blunt, produce "all talk, no action"? More broadly, some U.S. officials wondered whether key consultations and decisions on security matters might migrate over time from NATO, where America's unique political and military strengths ensure it has a preponderant role in shaping Alliance policies and operations, to the EU, where there is no U.S. seat at the table.

Oscar Wilde once observed, "There are many things that we would throw away if we were not afraid that others might pick them up." Perhaps Wilde's insight reflected the U.S. dilemma in trying to elicit greater European spending and effort in behalf of their own defense while at the same time seeming to refuse to take "yes" for an answer for fear of losing its influence over them. Fortunately, time and experience have improved U.S. as well as European understanding of ESDP's potential and limitations.

At the strategic level, one detects more convergent views on security threats to the Euro-Atlantic community. The *European Security Strategy* lists five key threats: terrorism; proliferation of WMD; regional conflict; state failure; and organized crime. Except for crime, the *U.S. National Security Strategy* of September 2002 and NATO's April 1999 *Strategic Concept* (as well as recent declarations) list essentially the same threats. The *European Security Strategy* emphasizes nonmilitary tools to prevent and diffuse crises but hardly strikes a pacifist stance. And to be fair, the *U.S. National Security Strategy* and NATO pronouncements recognize that states must use all their tools, not just the military, to meet 21st century threats.

When it comes to military capabilities, the EU seems to have become more realistic about its ambitions and pragmatic in its procedures. Its focus has shifted from the 1999 "Helsinki Headline Goal"—i.e., to develop by 2003 the ability to deploy up to 50,000-60,000 military personnel within 60 days and sustain them for at least 1 year on missions ranging from humanitarian and rescue tasks to peacekeeping and separating warring parties—to creating by 2007 a reservoir of 13 rapidly deployable 1,500-man "battle groups." According to EU plans, two of these battle groups should be able to undertake concurrent operations, normally under a UN mandate, lasting 1 to 4 months. The EU has pledged to make its battlegroup concept complementary and mutually reinforcing with NATO's significantly more capable Response Force—a U.S. initiative endorsed by NATO leaders at their Prague Summit in 2002.

Much remains be done to improve EU military capabilities, but the fundamental logic of close cooperation with NATO is now obvious. Of the 25 EU members, 19 are in NATO and 4 are in NATO's Partnership for Peace (PfP). Each has a single army, air force, navy, and defense budget to meet NATO, EU, and national commitments. There is no margin for wasteful duplication, and divergent operational doctrines and practices would increase the inherent risks in military operations.

The proof of ESDP's worth will rest with its performance on missions. On balance, its record so far has been positive, as the EU launched a police mission in Bosnia in January 2003 (complementing the NATO-led Stabilization Force, known as SFOR); assumed a small follow-on mission from NATO in Macedonia 2 months later; and conducted a 3-month "autonomous" operation (led by French forces) in the Democratic Republic of the Congo during the summer of 2003. On December 2, 2004, NATO-EU cooperation began a more critical test in Bosnia when NATO terminated its successful 9-year-old SFOR mission, and the EU deployed a new military mission, ALTHEA. NATO provides important support to ALTHEA under the NATO-EU "Berlin Plus" arrangements finalized in March 2003, and the Alliance will remain engaged with Bosnia through a NATO headquarters in Sarajevo. The United States has fully supported this transition.

In each of these major areas—i.e., EU strategy, capabilities, and operations—one can find evidence of a positive UK influence. (Here I refer to the "UK" in the broadest sense of the term, meaning its government's positions as well as the role played by very able UK nationals serving in NATO and EU structures.) This is not to suggest, however, that U.S.-EU or NATO-EU relations are or will be problem-free. NATO and the EU remain profoundly different in vision (NATO, for example, does not aspire to "ever closer union"), structure, scope, and procedures, despite many shared democratic values and security interests. Awkward moments between them are inevitable. Thus, one should not expect the United States to adopt an essentially *laissez-faire* attitude toward ESDP or to continue to rely on the UK as heavily as it might have in the past to "protect" U.S. security interests insofar as they might be affected by EU actions.

For the most part, I would not expect to see significant differences between Washington and London over the more theoretical—if not theological—question of whether the EU should seek to become a "counterweight" to the U.S. "hyperpower" or a new grand actor in a "multipolar" world. Instead, I could foresee a continuing series of irritations arising from seemingly disparate and (in some instances) second-tier issues that take on a life of their own and, over time, begin to have a corrosive effect on the special relationship.

Take, for example, the long-standing U.S. concerns (which predate the current administration) with the slow pace of European efforts to address acknowledged shortfalls in areas such as deployability; mobility; C4ISR; precision strike; sustainment; and chemical, biological, radiological, and nuclear defenses. Arguably, UK voices were more influential than those of other EU members in assuring American officials—some of whom were predisposed to be skeptical—that the EU "label" could mobilize serious European capabilities development in a way that NATO could not (at least, not alone.) However, nearly 6 years into ESDP, it is not easy to find a significant boost in real European capabilities attributable to the EU. The NATO-EU "Capabilities Group," which the United States had hoped would be an important vehicle for building a close, cooperative, and transparent relationship between the two organizations in this crucial area, has been a serious disappointment.

One could cite other areas of palpable American disappointment, as well, including:

- The emergence (albeit nascent and incremental) of an EU operational planning capability that would appear to duplicate some of the planning functions of NATO's Supreme Headquarters Allied Powers, Europe (SHAPE) (seemingly in contradiction to earlier European assurances);

- The festering stalemate over establishing useful NATO liaison arrangements within the EU Military Staff, with a reciprocal EU liaison at SHAPE;

- The apparently substantial and growing sentiment within the EU that the "Berlin Plus" arrangements used in the transition from the NATO-led SFOR mission to the EU's Operation ALTHEA in Bosnia have proved so cumbersome that the EU should seek to avoid their use in the future (seeming to contradict the general view within NATO); and,

- The absence of a sustained, multilevel, and strategic dialogue between NATO and the EU on issues that should be of mutual concern, such as Russia, Ukraine, the Caucasus, and African flash points.

To be clear, this is not to suggest that the UK is primarily responsible for difficulties in these or other areas. Various other actors within the EU and NATO have taken turns—some with demonstrably more *élan* than others—at erecting obstacles in the way of what logically should be a cooperative and mutually reinforcing relationship. The impression remains, however, that the UK might not, or cannot, or perhaps does not intend to "deliver" on every issue where U.S. or broader NATO interests reasonably should be taken into account.

On the one hand, Americans should not find this particularly shocking. The UK, like other EU members, has a number of interests at stake within that structure at any one time. Depending on circumstances and, in some cases, personalities, compromises might be necessary on some ESDP-related issues in order to better defend UK interests in non-ESDP areas. The notion of "horse trading" is not foreign to the U.S. Congress or Executive Branch, and even a casual observer of the EU must conclude that the "Old Continent" is just as practiced at it. The point remains, however, that when the UK does line up with EU partners in ways that appear to promote an "EU caucus" within NATO or to contradict or sidestep bilateral assurances to Washington, it is not only U.S. confidence in the EU as a body that is likely to suffer.

Although not an ESDP issue per se, the U.S.-EU imbroglio over the possible lifting of the EU embargo on arms sales to China should serve as a chilling example of how the special relationship could suffer as a result of EU decisions. Fortunately, this impending train wreck was avoided — or at least deferred. Hopefully, U.S., UK, and other EU members will develop a future "strategic dialogue" on China and avoid the transfer of potentially destabilizing capabilities and technologies, which would incite Congress — perhaps with at least tacit administration support — to enact some type of punitive and ultimately counterproductive legislation.

Over the longer term, I believe the United States needs to consider such steps as the following:

- We should look at developing an approach to ESDP that puts greater emphasis on advance consultations with a broad range of individual EU members and, increasingly, with various staffs and structures within the EU. In other words, we should put less reliance on the special relationship to gain understanding into evolving attitudes within the EU before the EU's positions are fixed and to explain U.S. perspectives and potential concerns. As Under Secretary of State for Political Affairs Burns recently noted, the United States has agreed to EU High Representative Javier Solana's suggestion to upgrade the "U.S.-EU Senior Level Group," a forum for high-level policy dialogue on a range of political and strategic issues. This is a step in the right direction.

- In parallel, we also should try to better understand EU procedures, decisionmaking timelines, the interrelationship between ESDP and non-ESDP issues, and where those fall in terms of the relative priorities of various EU members. To accomplish this, we probably will need to reexamine how we are organized — in Washington, our European embassies, and our NATO and EU missions — to better identify, track, and decide whether (and if so, how) to seek to influence (in a positive sense!) EU decisions on ESDP issues of interest.

- In this context, one might consider a more routine, extensive, and substantive program of "embedding" UK diplomats and military officers in appropriate State Department and

Pentagon staffs, with reciprocal arrangements for American diplomats and officers in the Foreign and Commonwealth Office and Ministry of Defence. This would pay dividends for both the special relationship and, more broadly, U.S.-EU relations.

These are not trivial steps, but I think they can be accomplished in time without falling into the trap of appearing to play off some Europeans against others — an occasional tactic that would be a disaster if elevated to an underlying strategy. I also think this can be done without prejudice to U.S. relations with NATO, which will remain the primary U.S. link to European security issues for the foreseeable future.

It is encouraging, in this regard, that after meeting with fellow Alliance leaders during his February 2005 visit to Brussels, President Bush traveled downtown to become the first American President to meet the European Council, Presidency, and College of Commissioners in the symbolic home of European integration. His remarks during that trip clearly indicate that the United States wants to deepen cooperation with its European allies and partners in both organizations, and to strengthen NATO-EU links, as well. Such a U.S., UK, and EU *ménage à trois* will not be a quick or easy affair, but it is incumbent upon the entire transatlantic community — and, of course, the special relationship — to nudge the relationship along.

ENDNOTES - CHAPTER 11

1. *National Defense Strategy* is available at *http://www.defenselink.mil/news/ Mar2005/d20050318nds1.pdf*. *National Security Strategy* is available at— *http://www. whitehouse.gov/nsc/nss.html.*

2. *National Military Strategy.*

3. See statement of General James Jones before Senate Armed Services Committee on March 1, 2005, available at *http://www.eucom.mil/Command/Posture/ Released%20-%20EUCOM%20FY%2006%20SASC%20Posture%20Statement%201 %20Mar%2005).doc.*

4. *Ibid.*

5. See *http://www.mod.uk/issues/security/cm6269/index.html.*

6. Then Secretary of State for Defence Hoon announced the creation of a new "special reconnaissance regiment" in April 2005.

7. Briefing by Assistant Secretary of Defense, Dr. J. D. Crouch, on Nuclear Posture Review, January 9, 2002, available at *http://www.defenselink.mil/ transcripts/2002/t01092002_t0109npr.html*.

8. Harold Macmillan, *At the End of the Day*, Harper & Row, New York, 1973, p. 360.

9. *Ibid.*, p. 359.

10. *Ibid.*, p. 357.

11. This section draws on the work of my INSS colleague, Ms. Elaine Bunn. See her paper, "Deploying Missile Defense: Major Operational Challenges," *Strategic Forum*, No. 209, August 2004, available at *http://www.ndu.edu/inss/strforum/SF209/ SF209.pdf*.

CHAPTER 12

THE DEFENSE DIMENSION
OF THE ANGLO-AMERICAN SPECIAL RELATIONSHIP

Charles Dick

A Historical Perspective.

In the 19th century, there was no particular warmth in interstate relations between Britain and the United States. There was one, albeit short, war between them and periodic tensions. The United States continued to follow the advice of the founding fathers and avoided "entangling alliances," concentrating on western hemispheric concerns.[1] The United Kingdom (UK) devoted its energies to the empire and the maintenance of a balance of power in Europe. Even World War I, when both countries fought a common foe, did not bring the two noticeably closer together. Indeed, American hostility to colonialism and the British exploitation of victory to expand their empire left relations decidedly cool. Naval rivalry exacerbated this coolness. The British soon realized they could not afford a naval race and had to reach an accommodation on American terms, but neither this nor the abandonment of the Anglo-Japanese alliance modified the U.S. view that Britain was essentially a wicked colonial oppressor fundamentally at odds with American idealism. Even the growing threat of fascism failed to shift the United States away from a disapproving isolationism born of disillusionment with the Versailles settlement.

The "special relationship" was a product of the combined endeavor to defeat Nazi Germany and Imperial Japan. In origin, it was thus a relatively recent phenomenon. Moreover, the close wartime relationship, often stormy as a result of disagreements over strategy, masked continuing differences over the desired nature of the postwar world. Initially, as if little had changed, the UK reverted to the pursuit of national interest—a Mediterranean strategy and the maintenance of empire (though American wartime and postwar actions had fatally undermined Britain's economic capacity for independent action). By contrast, with the adoption of the Truman Doctrine, the United States accepted that everything had changed. Containment of communism became the guiding principle of American foreign policy. As Britain, too, favored containment, cooperation continued, for instance over the defense of Greece and Korea and in the formation of the North Atlantic Treaty Organization (NATO). However, different perceptions of national interests clashed in the Middle East. Imperial strategy led the British and French into the Suez intervention of 1956, an adventure successfully foiled by a United States impelled by a differing view of the Egyptian regime and visceral anti-colonialism.

The British learned a painful lesson from Suez: the postwar UK lacked the economic basis necessary to give substance to its pretensions as a global power. Britain could no longer act globally without U.S. support. Henceforth, the UK would eschew independent action and direct its efforts to binding Europe and the United States together in common defense and security policies to face down the emerging Soviet threat.[2] As British power and influence steadily became more threadbare and the retreat from empire accelerated, Britain clung ever more closely to the United States. It argued, to itself as much as to other powers, that its influence over America, stemming from the special relationship, still gave it the status of a great power — a status underscored by its possession of a nuclear deterrent (even though the independent nature of its force soon became illusory as it became dependent on the United States for its delivery system).

The special relationship thus assumed a central place in London's worldview and strategy. It was not mirrored in Washington. The United States was a genuine world power, pursuing a global mission and interests. In doing so, it would cooperate with the UK where that was advantageous, for example in NATO and over the Falklands dispute. But where national interest dictated, it would cheerfully ignore Britain. Actually it was apparently a close call whether or not it would side with Argentina in 1982, and in the next year America trumped up an excuse to invade a Commonwealth country, Grenada, without so much as a word to its closest ally.

Nevertheless, the special relationship had substance during the Cold War as both parties shared a common, and overriding, strategic goal. While differing over some issues, for instance the desirability of closer European integration (favored by Washington, resisted in London), the two countries were happy to work together to give leadership and coherence to a sometimes wavering NATO. Of course, the United States gave the direction and Britain gave it loyal support. However, the end of the Cold War revealed important latent differences in national interests and in attitudes to problems. On a whole range of issues, from how to deal with the break-up of Yugoslavia, through the Israeli-Palestinian dispute and intrusive verification of the Chemical and Biological Weapons (CBW) convention to climate change and the importance of international law and organizations (to name but five), Britain found itself at odds with America. Britain was also finding that its relationship was not so special that it could significantly influence U.S. policy on many issues dear to its government's heart. American exceptionalism and unilateralist tendencies, never wholly dormant even during the Cold War years, were now proving singularly resistant to outside opinion, including that of the most loyal U.S. ally.

It is clear that the 40-year-old Anglo-American special relationship was a product of specific Cold War circumstances and based on a common need. The ending of those circumstances and needs is progressively revealing major differences in policy. The United States has global interests and aspirations that are not always shared by Britain. It could also be added that the relationship was never based on mutual admiration; for cultural and historical reasons, each partner traditionally has felt a measure of indifference, even condescension and disdain, for the other.

The British Perspective Today on the Defense Relationship.

During the Cold War, U.S. armed forces were far and away the most potent of those arrayed in NATO. Nevertheless, several European powers fielded significant military capabilities to meet the common threat. Those days are over. The implosion of the Warsaw Pact and the collapse of Russian power led all European countries to pay themselves large peace dividends (Britain, for instance, reduced the personnel strength of its armed forces from 315,000 to 210,000). Most European countries now maintain anachronistic militaries of limited relevance to the security and defense needs of the early 21st century. And most have a strategic vision which extends little beyond the continent of Europe. The only notable exceptions are France and, particularly, the UK.

Britain is striving, though with greatly reduced resources, to maintain a full spectrum of capabilities. The emphasis on force restructuring has moved from meeting a defined threat to Europe to an international role in a disorderly world. The stress is now on expeditionary operations in a multilateral environment, doing everything from peace support through nation-building to warfighting — i.e., engagement across the entire spectrum of conflict. And when the British consider multilateral operations, they mean primarily in conjunction with the United States. British defence efforts are geared to ensuring that its armed forces can work intimately with, and under the command of, American formations.

This British approach to defense reflects the conviction of Prime Minister Tony Blair that Britain must conduct an active foreign policy, when necessary reinforcing it with armed intervention, to make the world a safer and better place. As the UK can do relatively little on its own, this will require close cooperation with a similarly activist United States. This, in turn, reflects — and dovetails nicely with — the primary aim of foreign policy as set out by Blair in his definitive address to British ambassadors in January 2003 — that Britain should remain America's closest ally (in the hope and expectation that the United States would reciprocate). In June of that year, then Defence Secretary Geoffrey Hoon echoed his master's words, setting out the assumptions that guide his department's work:

- there is a moral requirement for Britain's armed forces to be a force for good in the world;

- the reality is that, in all but minor affairs, little can be accomplished without help from the Americans, who will participate only if they lead;

- the special relationship is the bedrock of British foreign policy, and, to sustain it, the country must be prepared to pay a price, including blood, to prove that it is the most dependable U.S. ally;

- UK defense gains much from close association with America; and,

- loyalty and reliability gain Britain significant influence in Washington.

Accepting that the assumptions above still hold sway, there is much to be said in favor of Hoon's analysis. On the other hand, the conclusions he draws are open to question; so, too, given resource restraints, is the ability of Britain's armed forces to meet the challenge that he lays down.

To start with capabilities, it is certainly true that Britain gains much from defense cooperation with, and help from, the United States. It enhances the effectiveness of British forces and thus the ability of the country to "punch above its weight." All three armed services, but especially the Navy and Air Force, are better off for their privileged access to American technology, and Britain's defense industries are closely tied to, perhaps even dependent on, their links with their American counterparts. Like its predecessor, Britain's nuclear force (now the *Trident* system) was purchased on the cheap from America and is dependent on the United States to keep it going.

Britain also profits from intelligence cooperation. The intelligence relationship goes back over 60 years (and cooperation continued even during periods of wider policy disagreements). Until the explosion of American investment in intelligence collection during the Cold War, especially in outer space (which the UK could not match), Britain led the field. Even today, its expertise in analysis in the areas of imagery intelligence (IMINT), signals intelligence (SIGINT), and technical intelligence (TECHINT) makes a significant contribution to the joint endeavor. But there can be no doubt that, deprived of uniquely privileged access to the fruits of American collection efforts, Britain would be critically lacking in situational awareness.

While Britain undeniably gains more than it contributes to the defense relationship, a critical question for the country is how important its contribution to the United States is. In many ways the answer depends, at least in part, on how much influence Britain can exert on American decisionmaking. Is British support essential to America in the defense field, or is it now merely a nice-to-have add-on?

It is certainly important *politically*, for instance, by providing a fig leaf of multilateralism to cover the nakedness of American unilateralism in launching the invasion of Iraq. The UK is also valuable to the United States as a stable and reliable base and site for missile early warning systems. But despite the wishful thinking, indeed boasting, of most politicians and journalists and some military men, the harsh reality appears to be that British participation is not highly valued in purely *military* terms. In a few niche areas, such as intelligence, mine clearance, photo reconnaissance, and special operations, the contributions are indeed important. However, the Royal Navy and Air Force as a whole are seen to be perilously close to critical mass and add little of significance to American strength. Similarly, in the realm of ground forces, any British contribution is somewhat marginal; numbers often still matter, as the Iraqi insurgency is demonstrating anew, and the Army lacks them.

Consequently, British influence on American military doctrinal development is marginal — at least unless and until events prove the former's ideas to be superior. Similarly, in both the 1991 and 2003 attacks on Iraq, while the British had an impact on tactical planning, their say in defining the end state and in campaign planning was minimal. There was no reestablishment of the wartime Combined Chiefs of Staff committee. British involvement was not critical to American success.

The level of influence exerted on the United States at the policy level is rather more difficult to assess. Historically, it has waxed and waned according to the international situation and the personalities involved. Certainly, the British self-image of wise and discerning, if not strong, Greeks guiding the powerful but naïve and ignorant Romans was always, and is now more than ever, a product of wishful thinking rather than fact.[3] If appearances are anything to go by, the UK's staunchly Atlanticist stance, even when it has cost the government dear (as over Iraq today), has given it little discernible influence in Washington in the post-Cold War era. For political reasons, not least to legitimize American actions, the British are considered useful to have alongside. But the United States does not consider it necessary to pay much of a price for the privilege. Rather, Washington seems to calculate that London will always come "on side" eventually, so no concessions are necessary. The UK tends to be taken for granted, like the loyal sidekick to the hero so beloved in Hollywood movies. Thus, for instance, President Bill Clinton undermined British policy over the wars of Yugoslav succession and interfered egregiously in the internal affairs of the UK over the Northern Ireland problem. President George W. Bush has conceded little or nothing to Prime Minister Blair over issues dear to the latter's heart, such as involvement of the United Nations (UN) in the invasion of Iraq, combating climate change, the International Criminal Court, and the way in which the Israeli-Palestinian problem should be approached. These examples rather suggest that the special relationship has not survived the end of the Cold War in a fashion palatable to a UK that seeks to promote its own national interests.

The imbalance in capabilities is likely to grow as it is unlikely that the Defence Secretary and the British military can achieve their ambition of fully taking up and exploiting the advanced technologies produced by the latest revolution in military affairs. Costs are forever spiralling, often logarithmically, and increased spending on defense is not electorally rewarding these days. To compound the problem, the government will soon have to decide on whether or not to purchase a *Trident* replacement. If, as seems most likely, it decides that Britain should remain a nuclear power, the cost of any new system will have to be met at the expense of conventional forces as new money will not be in the offing. What value the United States attaches to British military assistance rests solely on the latter's conventional forces. British *Tridents* are irrelevant to American defense and security.

This problem of defense spending may become more acute if the British public becomes progressively more disillusioned as a result of the Iraq war and insurgency and with the government's interventionist proclivities. Moreover, however unfairly, there is a widespread perception that Blair is merely Bush's poodle, and fighting in what is widely regarded as a bad cause to pull Bush's chestnuts out of the fire is not popular. Given the unfavorable impression generated by the war and other high-handed, unilateral actions, anti-Americanism is on the rise in the UK, both on the right and left of politics. This perspective may grow more rapidly in the aftermath of the suicide bombings in London in July 2005. As a result, this may well act as a constraint on future combined operations. It may also undermine public support for the defense establishment's desire to ensure interoperability with the American armed forces.

Another factor brought to the fore by the Iraq war and other American saber rattling also limits the perceived usefulness of a British commitment to fighting alongside the United States. There are considerable transatlantic differences in interpretation of the role of, importance of, adherence to, and development of international law. What Hoon called "lawfare" can dominate British military planning in a way that mystifies the Americans. Just as the United States tired of managing war by committee during the Kosovo conflict in 1999 when countries making a negligible military commitment insisted on exercising influence on the conduct of operations, so they might come to deprecate British insistence on perceived legal niceties.

All in all, Britain's practical usefulness to the United States in the military field may well decline in the future (though its significance as a forward base will not). Britain may also cease to play its once valuable role as champion of U.S. policies within NATO. European members are mostly reluctant to expand the charter of the alliance much beyond the narrow confines agreed in 1949, and some favor the creation of a European Union (EU) military force that is not dependent on America. Increasingly, for its part, the United States favors *ad hoc* coalitions of the willing over working within the confines of an alliance in which most members are seen not to be pulling their weight. A combination of reducing conventional strength and political influence in NATO would lead to a diminution of the already small influence that London can exert in Washington.

Should Britain Remain in the Nuclear Club?

The original decision to acquire a nuclear capability was made in response to a perceived growth of anti-British and isolationist sentiment in the United States. The acquisition of an atomic bomb in 1952 and of a hydrogen bomb in 1958 was seen as restoring the country fully to the ranks of the great powers. However, the UK possessed a genuinely independent nuclear deterrent for only 10 years. With the purchase, on very favorable terms, of the *Polaris* system in 1962, Britain became dependent on the United States to keep its deterrent functioning. However, as then Prime Minister Harold Macmillan put it, *Polaris* solved the "problem of being poor and powerful at the same time." The same rationale underlay the acquisition of *Trident* in the early 1980s, the British *Chevaline* warhead having proved both too expensive and not good enough as an upgrade to the existing system.

Dependence on America to keep the nuclear "show on the road" was not seen to be a major weakness. Solidarity in the face of the Soviet threat made that vulnerability mainly theoretical. And if war were to come, the Union of Soviet Socialist Republics (USSR) might calculate that, when the chips were down, the United States might hesitate to risk nuclear immolation in retaliation for attacks on Europe. But it would be far less certain about the actions of a Britain that was more or less in the front line.

The British government accepts that the issue of a *Trident* replacement has to be resolved in the current parliament. In its election manifesto, the Labour Party committed itself to retaining a nuclear deterrent. Now that the Soviet threat has gone, however, the case for retention is far weaker. Proponents put forward several arguments:

- Britain should keep a nuclear capability as an insurance policy in an uncertain world;
- being a nuclear power confers prestige and is almost the sole rationale for Britain's continued holding of a permanent, veto-wielding seat on the UN Security Council; and,
- Britain cannot allow France to be the sole European nuclear power.

These rationales are not wholly convincing. It is hard indeed to envisage a situation where Britain could alone face an enemy deterrable with nuclear weapons—certainly a terrorist group armed with weapons of mass destruction (WMD) could not be intimidated in the same way that a state can be. If countries facing a real threat, such as Germany and Japan during the Cold War, felt able to rely on American extended deterrence, why should not Britain do the same in less threatening times? Could the United States really remain indifferent to a serious military threat to Britain? A very expensive insurance policy against an unspecifiable danger is not worth paying if the cost of the premium means that you cannot afford the upkeep of real essentials. Any new nuclear system can be purchased only at the expense of conventional capabilities that will assuredly be needed—if only to sustain the special defense relationship with the United States.

Does the British semi-independent nuclear deterrent provide the only justification for membership in the Security Council nuclear club? Does Britain's activeness in the UN, particularly in peacekeeping and peace enforcement (both dependent on conventional armed forces) count for so little? In any case, membership in the nuclear club is no longer seen as a *sine qua non* of membership, now that the admission of other powers is under active consideration. In any event, the question arises once again, Is the cost too high? As to the French, how much leverage does their *force de frappe* really confer in today's world? The cost of its maintenance certainly acts as a drag on developing a modern conventional capability. And would it really be to Britain's disadvantage if France were Europe's sole nuclear power?

If it is deemed truly essential that Britain remain a nuclear player, it is to be hoped that the country pays the lowest possible stake to remain in the game. Another submarine-based system would put an impossible strain on the defense budget, even if the Americans waived the research and development (R&D) costs as they did with *Trident*. Cruise missiles such as *Tomahawk* would provide a cheap and cheerful—and dual-capable—alternative that should be adequate to deal with any threat Britain is likely to face. Alternatively, it could be worth pursuing an Anglo-French project. While France has showed no interest in the past in nuclear pooling, it, too, feels the cost of maintaining an independent system and could perhaps be induced to come in with the UK if the latter were seen to be making a genuine effort to put life into a European defense identity and capability.

Britain's Future Strategic Direction.

Even after the disappearance of the Soviet threat, Britain and other European countries still have plenty of security interests and problems in common with the United States. These, as well as bureaucratic inertia, help to explain the continued existence of

NATO despite the decay of danger from the east. All are concerned about:

- WMD proliferation;
- international terrorism, especially of the messianic and/or nihilistic variety;
- the prevalence of ethnic/religious conflict and its potential impact on wider stability;
- organized crime, especially narcotics and people trafficking; and,
- the emergence of weak and failing states and the possibility that they will become (as Afghanistan and others have done) havens for terrorists and criminal enterprises.

However, the states of mainland Europe are reluctant to raise their strategic vision beyond their own continent. They have little appetite for committing NATO to "out of area" tasks and less for funding serious military capabilities to do so. They may bemoan developments such as the apparent Iranian threat to acquire nuclear weapons or the seemingly never-ending Israeli-Palestinian struggle, but they are not willing to go beyond aid and diplomacy (not backed by military power) in attempting to find answers. Things are different in the United States. As a result of the ending of the Cold War, the eclipse of Russian power, and, especially, the galvanizing effect of the September 11, 2001 (9/11), atrocity, America has apparently decided to pursue global hegemony, not, of course, for its own sake but as the only doable way to solve worldwide problems. It sees itself as a benign hegemon, one whose dominance and decisions are, by definition, good for all save so-called rogue states and other criminal and anti-democratic regimes. America seems determined to reshape the world in a way congenial to it, and in doing so not to be bound by any restrictions such as antiquated notions of international law. Rather it will follow its own judgments.

Most Europeans, save for the former Soviet satellites, distrust American ambitions, even motives. To an extent, especially with the French, this stems from the inevitable resentment against the now sole superpower—exacerbated by America's egregious lack of sensitivity to the needs and opinions of others. There are, however, more substantive factors inhibiting the relatively close collaboration that characterized the Cold War era:

- not all American interests and problems are seen as European ones too, e.g., the increasing capability of China's military and the threat to Taiwan—indeed most developments in the Far East;

- where they are held in common, perceptions of their causes and cures often differ, as with the Israeli-Palestinian conflict and its significance for the struggle against international terrorism, not to mention the way in which that struggle is conducted; and,

- while most values, like adherence to democratic norms, are shared, there are important differences—for instance over the central role and importance of international law and institutions in finding solutions to international problems.

This divergence of interests and, even when they coincide, of approaches between the United States and much of the EU, including its most influential members, is now causing a problem for the UK. Ever since the Suez debacle illustrated the hollowness of Britain's great power pretensions, the first principle of British foreign policy has been that Britain remains the closest ally of the United States. As noted earlier, Prime Minister Blair reiterated this line as recently as 2003 in his speech to British ambassadors. In the same speech, however, he maintained that the country must also be at the heart of Europe. "Britain must be at the centre of Europe . . . . It will grow in power. To separate ourselves from it would be madness." He asserts that there is no incompatibility between the two aims. Britain can, and must, be a transatlantic bridge between the two (also a self-assigned task of previous prime ministers and always greatly resented by French and German leaders).

However much Blair believes (or pretends) that there is no contradiction between looking simultaneously west and east, the Iraq war and other contentious issues have blown the idea apart. The depth of acrimony and bitterness that has developed between the United States and the traditional leaders of Europe will not be overcome easily or quickly, whatever soothing words are spoken to paper over the cracks. Moreover, America is working to strengthen ties with former communist, and more Atlanticist, central European countries (especially those with large resident U.S. minorities) rather than cultivating what U.S. Defense Secretary Donald Rumsfeld contemptuously dismissed as "old Europe." Clearly, the United States has abandoned its decades-old efforts to encourage a more closely integrated and therefore stronger Europe (a policy which used to cause much consternation in London. It no longer needs a stronger European arm of NATO to balance the USSR and fears that a stronger EU will be less malleable, perhaps even a competitor. America now seeks to divide and rule NATO, even the EU, and this will exacerbate divisions which have already come to light in several areas. Ideas and interests are diverging in several important areas of policy, and these differences will probably inhibit cooperation, even over issues where there is actually much common ground. Both sides of the Atlantic will demand that Britain choose between them. Persisting with a third way is an illusion, not an option.

What should be the UK's choice of strategic direction? Should the country continue to follow its traditional, hitherto immutable policy and cleave to the United States, clinging to a special relationship that has lost most of its substance with the end of the Cold War that sustained it? Or should it recognize and accept the realities of geography and economic interest and genuinely put itself at the heart of Europe? In essence, it is a choice between accepting the status of a U.S. satellite — Britain can never aspire to be more than a nominal partner — and being a shaping power in Europe where its weight would give it real influence.[4]

Actually, the present Labour government (and any near-future Conservative alternative) is all but certain to duck the issue and continue sitting on the fence, insisting that the choice is artificial and need not be made. Governments hate to make hard choices, especially on such an issue as this with all the obfuscatory myths, false perspectives, chauvinistic sentiments, prejudices, and uncertainties that surround it. Adhering thus to the continuing balancing act will be interpreted in Europe as a *de facto* continuation of the America-first policy. Whatever its other benefits, it will cost the country dear in the EU, as it has done for the last 40 years since De Gaulle's first veto on membership in the European Economic Community (EEC).

Quite apart from French and others' fears that Britain will act as a Trojan horse for the United States in its aim to divide and rule, there will always remain the fear that, when the chips are down, Britain will abandon its European partners in favor of its transatlantic ally. A country with such a suspicion hanging over it can never aspire to a leadership role.

Such an outcome would probably be bad for the entire western world, not least in the realm of security and defense. As the Iraq entanglement and other contemporary issues are making clear, even the uniquely powerful United States cannot resolve every problem on its own. Indeed, overstretch in one area will weaken its ability to exercise decisive influence in others—as is arguably happening today in the cases of Iran and North Korea. Nor can Washington rely on a tame NATO to do its bidding. The cement that held the alliance together, a common fear of the USSR, has lost its power to bind and has not been replaced by a commitment to new missions. The Americans seem to have lost patience with NATO politics and its toothlessness and relegated it to a minor role. They seem to wish it to continue as the primary defense institution for Europeans mainly because it gives them a say in European affairs, and it prevents the emergence of any European decisional independence. The Europeans, for their part, seem content with shuffling deck chairs instead of facing new realities.

The Americans would benefit from the creation of an effective European security and defense policy backed by a strong military arm, to share burdens where agreement exists. Problems will arise in which the United States will not wish for involvement. There will be others for which, thanks to commitments elsewhere, America cannot find the resources to intervene. An EU force might be able to fill the breach. There would indubitably be disagreements between a strong EU and the United States, but, given fundamental values and interests that are shared, these can be resolved, as they currently are in the area of trade where the EU is now a power to be reckoned with. A militarily powerful EU need not be a rival to America, or to a NATO which will in any case always be ineffectual without the participation of the principal EU players. On the contrary, in most security and defense issues, it could and should be complementary.

It has been persuasively argued that an effective European defense organization is a pipe dream. It may well be so. Two things are reasonably certain, though.

- Effective European defense is much more likely to happen if Britain abandons its semi-detached attitude to the EU and offers genuine commitment and leadership. Many countries would welcome a lead from a major player that possesses a well-respected military and is neither burdened with the sins of the past nor driven by a visceral anti-Americanism.

- If Britain remains cool towards the project but it nevertheless progresses, it will most likely do so under French direction. France, the EU's other serious military power, would seek to make it a rival to, rather than an effective partner for, the United States.

With the St Malo declaration of 1998, it appeared that Britain was shifting from its reluctance to contemplate any defense initiative outside NATO and was prepared, together with France, to give substance to a European security and defense identity. The two governments agreed that the EU "must have a capacity for autonomous action, backed up by credible military forces, the means to decide to use them and the readiness to do so."[5] At the same time, however, they both accepted that "the Atlantic Alliance is the foundation of Europe's collective security." Has the acrimony resulting from the split over Iraq and other nondefense-related issues made it impossible to return to this promising road? Has the embarrassment and shame resulting from the exposure of Europe's incapacity to act without reliance on the Americans over Bosnia and Kosovo been forgotten? Or can the EU still get its act together and assemble a military capability that somewhat matches its economic strength? Obviously, this question looms particularly large in the aftermath of the rejection of the draft EU constitution by French and Dutch voters.

With Britain at least sharing the helm, European defense would not be defined by opposition to the United States in some zero-sum game. Cooperation wherever and whenever possible would be the goal, though the EU would not act as a mere satellite of America.

Recognizing this, the United States would not, it is to be hoped, "cut off its nose to spite its face" by severing its often close relationship with the UK. After all, America gains something from it, too, and it would still need a friend at the European court. Certainly, as a shaper and leader of a significant European security and defense effort, Britain would enjoy more influence in Washington than it does today as a loyal but unassertive ally that is too weak to compel attention. This would be a better outcome for Britain than being cold-shouldered in Europe and taken for granted in the United States.

ENDNOTES - CHAPTER 12

1. Ironically, America's Monroe Doctrine relied more on the dominance of the Royal Navy than on the power of the American fleet to dissuade intervention from the Old World.

2. Contrastingly, the French drew the lesson from Suez that the United States was an untrustworthy ally and that France needed to acquire the means to act independently. The difference in approach continues to this day.

3. This Greek-Roman analogy to describe the relationship between Britain and America was coined by Harold Macmillan, a future prime minister, in North Africa in 1943. It has been clung to ever since to rationalize and ease the pain of having to accept inferior status. And Britain's supposed influence over the superpower was regarded as increasing Britain's diplomatic weight.

4. Britain was faced with this choice as far back as 1957, when it chose an illusory great power status and the special relationship over membership in the fledgling EEC. Subsequent regrets, consequent on the collapse of traditional policy, led the UK belatedly to apply for membership, but this was blocked by a France mistrustful of British Atlanticism. The Edward Heath government, in a rare burst of Europe-first enthusiasm, succeeded in gaining entry in 1973. But by this time, the EEC had been shaped by France (mainly) and Germany in a fashion uncongenial to British interests.

5. To demonstrate British seriousness, the UK has offered 12,500 men, 18 ships, and 72 combat aircraft to give teeth to the new European Rapid Reaction Force. It also, however, resists (lest the Americans be upset) the establishment of an EU planning center at Tervuren, Belgium, separate from NATO.

CHAPTER 13

WHEN YOU COME TO A FORK IN THE ROAD, TAKE IT — DEFENSE POLICY AND THE SPECIAL RELATIONSHIP: PANEL CHAIRMAN'S REPORT

Jeffrey D. McCausland

The famous American philosopher and baseball player, Yogi Berra, once said that when you come to a fork in the road — take it. There is common agreement that Britain today finds itself at a juncture with respect to the defense aspects of the special relationship it has enjoyed with the United States since World War II. While leaders in America and the United Kingdom (UK) agree on this, it is curious that national defense and Anglo-American relations played practically no role in the 2005 British election. British politicians reflected the public's clear interest in immigration, healthcare, crime, and education. The defense panelists argued that in the aftermath of the reelection of both the American and British leaders, the United States must address four areas of fundamental importance if the special relationship is to flourish. These four areas are grand strategy, military operations, defense capabilities, and security organizations.

Prime Minister Tony Blair has on several occasions said that the role for Britain is to be closely allied with the United States *and* remain engaged in the heart of Europe.[1] He (like his predecessors) has argued repeatedly that the UK must be a bridge between the United States and continental Europe. But can the UK continue to perform this role in defense matters? This would seem daunting and perhaps even contradictory in a future that now requires reconsideration of the European Union (EU) Constitution, rejected by French and Dutch voters, as well as coping with a possible European desire to establish common approaches on defense and foreign policy. "Can Britain continue this triangular relationship or ménage a trois?"

Grand Strategy.

Strategy is the art of the possible. It requires successful management of three variables—ends, ways, and means. Consequently, any discussion of strategy and the special relationship must confront several fundamental questions. What is the end state—the politico-economic future—that American and British leaders are attempting to shape? And assuming they can agree on such a common vision, what are the defense policies best calculated to assist in its realization? And, finally, what are the means or resources both countries are able and willing to devote to this effort?

Throughout the history of national partnerships and alliances, the presence of a mutual threat has been fundamental to achieving agreement on strategy. Benjamin Franklin famously said upon signing the Declaration of Independence, "We now must all hang together or we will surely hang separately." The U.S.-UK relationship has "hung together" in the face of threats to national survival. Initially, the partners opposed imperial Germany, then confronted Hitlerian fascism, and finally faced down the threat posed by the Soviet Union and communism, acting in all three cases within the context of a broader alliance. During this time, the United States accepted the basic grand strategic principle that despite overwhelming American power, it needed allies for the capabilities they provided as well as the legitimacy gained from collective action. The two countries might have periodic severe disagreements over such issues as Suez, Vietnam, the Falklands, and Grenada, but both knew that the common threat was so great that reconciliation was likely, if not certain, in each case.

This common threat ended with the collapse of the Berlin Wall and demise of the Soviet Union. But in terms of defense links, the experience of 75 years established certain cooperative arrangements that are now routine and indeed taken for granted. These include unparalleled sharing of intelligence, regular consultations on military doctrine, American support for the UK nuclear deterrent, robust liaison teams in both the Pentagon and Ministry of Defence, and now British representation at several American regional combatant commands. Furthermore, American and British officers regularly cooperated on a host of issues at North Atlantic Treaty Organization

(NATO) headquarters and during conflicts in Iraq, Bosnia, and Kosovo over the past 20 years.

In the aftermath of September 11, 2001 (9/11), many in continental Europe, however, did not share the view that 9/11 changed the way in which America should perceive the world and evaluate threats. In spite of the attacks on Spain, Greece, Turkey, and now even London, it appears, from the American side of the Atlantic at least, that many Europeans still view 9/11 as fundamentally a U.S. problem that somehow Europe can avoid if it chooses. In terms of the special relationship, however, President George W. Bush observed following the attacks in London in July 2005, "Just as America and Great Britain stood together to defeat totalitarian ideologies of the 20th century, we now stand together against the murderous ideologies of the 21st century."[2]

Many Americans worry that continental Europe has failed to grasp the enormous impact 9/11 has had on the American psyche. As Leo Michel pointed out, the U.S. defense strategy as officially published by the Department of Defense (DoD) in March 2005 opens with the line: "America is a nation at war."[3] This view is not shared in Paris, Brussels, or Berlin. Consequently, will it be feasible for Britain to maintain its historical defense ties with the United States while working toward the greater European defense integration within the EU envisioned by the St. Malo agreement? How will British public attitudes be affected by the horrific events of July 2005?

Strategy begins with an analysis of threats, and Al Qaeda and its associated groups do not provide as coherent a face in this regard as did the Soviet Union. Both Britain and America agree on the threats posed by nuclear proliferation, cyber terrorism, weapons of mass destruction (WMD), bioterrorism, international crime, and failed states. But many in the UK were unsettled, and rightfully so, by America's "global war on terrorism" for its lack of definition. Many defense experts in both Britain *and* America have argued since 2001 that terrorism ultimately remains a technique as opposed to an enemy. Consequently, establishing a common grand strategy to confront terrorism as a shared threat is certainly challenging. Such a strategy must both reflect and cement public support for policies. In this regard, it is interesting to note that at least in the immediate aftermath of the London attacks, pro-U.S. feeling actually increased in some polls in the UK.[4]

Military Operations.

Cooperation between the American and British militaries is unparalleled not only with respect to U.S. relations with other states but perhaps even in the annals of alliances. No other state has the daily involvement in the planning and preparation of operations that the UK has with the United States. U.S. and British forces have cooperated well in Iraq and adapted quickly to the changing conditions on the ground as the war evolved from its initial conventional phase to counterinsurgency operations. Still, Charles Dick is correct when he observed that many in Britain worry that this cooperation may occur only at the tactical level. They are concerned that British influence on American thinking at the operational or higher levels is limited.

Both Washington and Whitehall should be concerned that "the coalition in Iraq is becoming less a coalition and more a clear partnership." The major European troop contributors to Iraq will remove their forces by the end of 2005. Outside NATO, there are no countries with sizable military forces lining up to assist. In Iraq, the January 2005 elections, continued training of indigenous security forces, and October 2005 referendum do, however, suggest that Britain and America may have at least reached the "end of the beginning." *But* continued domestic political progress along with sustained increases in the size and sophistication of Iraqi security forces will be crucial if the insurgency is to be defeated. Even the most optimistic analysts in both countries agree that a large-scale presence by the United States and UK in Iraq for the foreseeable future is inevitable. Plans exist, however, if these efforts are successful, for British forces to be cut in half by the end of 2006.[5] Even American troop commanders have spoken publicly about the possibility of significant U.S. troop reductions in 2006.

In every challenge lies the seeds of opportunity, and this may be the case now. American and British leaders should collectively seek greater assistance not in providing combat forces for Iraq, but in contributions particularly from European states in the training of Iraqi police, border guardsmen, and military forces. Some of the reports discussing a possible reduction of British forces in Iraq in 2006 suggest that this might result in a subsequent deployment by

British troops to Afghanistan to lead NATO forces in the south of that country.[6] Such a move would clearly enhance British efforts to be a bridge in the transatlantic relationship.

Defense Capabilities.

The eminent British historian Sir Michael Howard once observed that "capabilities lead to opportunities which lead to options and perhaps even intentions." This aphorism must remind us that vision without resources is a fairy tale. Here, both the United States and the UK confront major budgetary choices. As both Michel and Dick point out, at the top of the list may be the future of the British independent nuclear deterrent. The UK has managed to maintain its nuclear forces and the ability to project significant conventional forces abroad, even following the reductions that occurred as part of the peace dividend at the end of the Cold War. It remains to be seen whether the next government will be able to continue to do both in the face of spiraling costs for conventional forces and the need to replace the *Trident* nuclear force. Former Defence Secretary Geoffrey Hoon stated that the first principle of British defense planning is to be interoperable with the United States. Consequently, a fundamental question is, Should Britain retain an independent nuclear deterrent and, if so, for what strategic purpose? If the new government chooses to retain the nuclear deterrent, will there be sufficient remaining funds to transform British conventional forces for global deployment? Obviously, this problem has become even more complex following the July 2005 attacks in London that will likely demand far greater investments in homeland security.

In the aftermath of the 2005 elections, it appears that the Blair government intends to continue a British independent nuclear deterrent. John Reid, the new Defence Secretary, has opened talks with the United States on a successor to *Trident*. His government appears determined to maintain a British submarine-launched system because it is "invisible and invulnerable."[7] This represents an apparent shift from the earlier position, which seemed open to other less expensive options, such as ground or air-launched cruise missile systems. The full cost of developing the *Trident* replacement is estimated to be $25 billion to $35 billion. Such an investment would make even marginal increases in the size and continued technological improvements in conventional forces increasingly difficult.

The United States also faces tough budgetary choices, confronted as it is by the rising costs of the war in Iraq, demands for greater attention to homeland security, the mandate to transform U.S. forces, and the aftermath of natural disasters like Hurricane Katrina. As Michel pointed out, the U.S. administration must confront these choices in the ongoing *Quadrennial Defense Review* (QDR), scheduled for submission to Congress by February 2006.[8] It is interesting to note that representatives from the British military establishment are participating in the American QDR effort in Washington. Tellingly, DoD guidance for the QDR assumes no increase in American defense spending in the coming years.

Finally, Michel suggested that three other issues regarding defense capability deserve mention. The first is the American Global Restationing Plan. This will see a significant reduction of American forces in continental Europe while retaining, consistent with UK agreement, air bases in Great Britain. These bases, as well as the strategic British island of Diego Garcia, may in fact take on even greater importance to American defense planning. Second, the United States has begun the initial deployment of anti-ballistic missiles in Alaska and California. This process will continue with additional forces being readied for sea-based deployment in the near future. There has been close UK-U.S. cooperation on this effort, to include the establishment of an American radar system in Great Britain. Anglo-American discussions will continue on future UK participation in the ballistic missile defense system. This will not only require the two parties to determine costs and deployments, but also to establish an appropriate bilateral command and control mechanism for these forces. Third, with respect to defense industrial cooperation, there is a serious disconnect in the United States between the executive branch's longstanding desire for close defense and security cooperation with Great Britain (and a few others), on the one hand, and congressional restriction on foreign participation in U.S. defense programs, on the other.

Security Organizations.

As Dick observed, there has been a clear skepticism about the relevance of NATO in the Bush administration. This is due in part to the dramatic reductions in European defense spending over the past decade that have brought most European conventional forces to the brink of irrelevance. Such skepticism was demonstrated in the tepid acceptance of the NATO countries' offer to support the United States under Article V after 9/11 and continued with the very unfortunate comments by Secretary Donald Rumsfeld about "old Europe." Agreement exists among defense experts that Iraq has done severe structural damage to the transatlantic bridge. In this first year of the second Bush term, efforts were made by the United States to repair the relationship with NATO, consult more frequently, and use NATO not only as a source of military capability, but also as a collaborator through expanded discussions and planning. Time will tell whether such positive steps translate into improved relations.[9]

Still, it is worrisome to reflect on former German Chancellor Gerhard Schroeder's comments at Wehrkunde, Germany, in 2005 when he suggested that NATO may have outlived its usefulness and that a new organization needs to be envisaged to manage the transatlantic relationship. In many ways the Chancellor, now turning over the reins of government to Angela Merkel, may have been speaking less to the Americans than to the continental Europeans and the British. So what, then, is the future of NATO from the standpoint of the special relationship and what, collectively, should British and American leaders do to move the organization in the direction of relevancy?

In answering this question, existing NATO operations must also be taken into account. The Alliance conducted major out-of-area operation in the last decade. It still has significant forces *and* its credibility deployed in the Balkans. Unfortunately, the final political decision on the future of Kosovo has not yet been made, Montenegro's independence movement may yet be successful, and Macedonia will continue to confront enormous challenges. All of these unsettling situations could lead to a future crisis.[10] If another Balkans crisis occurs, two things might happen immediately. First, the United States, confronted by global overstretch, might well announce that the crisis is essentially a European problem. Second, this announcement would cause major problems for an already damaged transatlantic relationship.

Former U.S. Secretary of Defense Harold Brown and NATO Secretary General Lord George Robertson have broached another opportunity for Britain and America to provide leadership for the Alliance. Both have endorsed the need to create military capabilities and doctrine to take better advantage of network-based operations. They observed in a recent study that "the era of static, large, armored forces, in place to confront and deter the adversary's massed formations, is over. The era of forces that train and exercise together, but are rarely used, is over as well."[11]

A Final Word.

To mix metaphors, Britain may be at a fork in the road as it tries to be the transatlantic bridge as both shorelines threaten to recede. But the special relationship may itself be at a crossroads. There is a greater need than ever for reinvigorated consultation by leaders on a range of important issues that lie ahead *and* a need for leaders on both sides of the Atlantic to celebrate this relationship frequently and publicly. As we pass the 60th anniversary of the end of World War II, the current generation and those who focus on international politics are aware of the special relationship's value. But both countries must attempt to underscore its value more emphatically to their respective populations now and in future.

ENDNOTES - CHAPTER 13

1. For two excellent summaries, see Steven Kramer, "Blair's Britain After Iraq," *Foreign Affairs*, Vol. 88, Issue 4, July/August 2003, pp. 90; and Rodney Braithwaite, "End of the Affair," *Prospect*, May 2003, pp. 20-23.

2. Jim Vande Hei, "Bush Defends Strategy Against Terrorist Attacks," *New York Times*, July 12, 2005, p. A3.

3. Donald H. Rumsfeld, *The National Defense Strategy of the United States of America*, Washington, DC: Department of Defense, March 2005, p. 1.

4. Poll taken for the *Daily Telegraph*, London, July 8, 2004, by the YouGov Polling Firm, *www.YouGov.com*.

5. Victoria Burnett, Jimmy Burns, and Peter Spiegal, "MoD Plans Iraq Troop Withdrawal," *Financial Times*, July 2005, p. 1. See also Glenn Frankel and Josh White, "U.K. Memo Cites Plans for Troop Reduction," *Washington Post*, July 11, 2005, p. A01.

6. *Ibid.*

7. David Cracknell, "Talks Start With US on Trident's 15bn Successor," *London Sunday Times*, July 17, 2005, p. 1.

8. Thom Shanker and Eric Schmitt, "Pentagon Weighs Strategy Change to Deter Terror," *New York Times*, July 5, 2005, p. 1.

9. Ambassador Nicholas Burns, "A Trans Atlantic Agenda for the Year Ahead," remarks at Chatham House, London, April 6, 2005.

10. *Ibid.*

11. Guy Ben-Ari, "European Commitment to Network-Based Operations and the Transatlantic Doctrine Gap," *Initiative for a Renewed Transatlantic Partnership*, Washington, DC: Center for Strategic and International Studies, August 2005, p. 4.

CONCLUSION

CHAPTER 14

"WELL, ISN'T THAT SPECIAL?"
CONCLUDING REMARKS ON U.S.-UK RELATIONS
AT THE START OF THE 21st CENTURY

Douglas T. Stuart

I am sure that when some Americans hear the phrase "special relationship," their first reaction is to think of comedian Dana Carvey's "Church Lady." When Carvey's character is forced to confront some form of behavior or lifestyle which she disdains, she condescendingly replies: "Well, isn't that special?"

The Anglo-American special relationship is nothing to sneer, or sniff, at. It is extremely important to both the United States and the United Kingdom (UK). It has also been, and continues to be, an indispensable source of productive leadership for the international community.

On the other hand, the special relationship needs to be viewed realistically. Some of the contributors to this volume have highlighted instances in which fundamental differences of principle or interest have strained the Anglo-American relationship. In some cases, these disagreements have been exacerbated by unrealistic expectations. The most well-known example is the 1956 Suez crisis. The comments of Lieutenant General Sir Hugh Stockwell, commander of the British 1st Corps during the planning for the French-British-Israeli operation, illustrate the degree of misunderstanding on the UK side:

> . . . as the British could fairly claim a "special relationship" with the Americans, by which they would hope to maintain the neutrality of the United States in the period of operation, Britain was the obvious choice for leadership.[1]

London was not prepared for the intensely negative American response to the Suez invasion, nor for Secretary of State John Foster Dulles' subsequent explanation that the United States, which had extant defense arrangements with 44 other countries, "cannot have a hierarchy of relationships with allies around the world."[2] From the British point of view, a "hierarchy of relationships" was precisely the point.

Washington has also fallen prey to self-deluding fantasies from time to time. One example is Lyndon Johnson's efforts to convince Harold Wilson to contribute "a token force" to support America's beleaguered troops in Vietnam. The President argued that "a platoon of bagpipers would be sufficient."[3] By the time that Johnson made this request, however, Wilson's government was fully engaged in a campaign of retrenchment from East of Suez, and was unwilling to risk guilt by association with America's quixotic campaign in Southeast Asia. The fact that many Britons believed that the United States had contributed to the pressures which forced the UK to abandon its empire made Wilson's decision that much easier.

What is most interesting about the instances of disagreement and misunderstanding between the United States and the UK since World War II is their relative infrequency. In the overwhelming majority of cases when the two nations have taken international actions, they have acted either in unison or in harmony. Philip Stephens attributes this to a "deeply ingrained . . . habit of cooperation." But Nicholas Childs and Leo Michel remind us that this habit is reinforced by institutional arrangements which give the two governments preferential access to each other's intelligence and a "privileged" role in defense planning.

Gaining and retaining this special status has been a top priority for Britain since World War II. Indeed, Winston Churchill established this as a principle of British foreign policy even before the United States entered the war. In a statement before the House of Commons in 1940, he predicted that the two nations ". . . will have to be somewhat mixed up together" for the foreseeable future. He went on to reassure his colleagues, however, that "I do not view the process with any misgivings."[4] Churchill was, nonetheless, an unsentimental realist who understood that if London wanted to be treated by the United States as *primus inter pares*, it would have to provide more than sage advice and accumulated wisdom. As a result, all British governments since World War II have looked for ways to keep their nation militarily strong, not just as a good in itself but also as a means of sustaining the special relationship with the United States. The late

Brigadier Kenneth Hunt once described these efforts as a policy of "getting a quart out of a pint bottle" in the formulation of successive defense budgets.[5] For its part, the United States has helped Great Britain to manage this difficult task by various forms of bilateral defense cooperation, including nuclear-sharing arrangements.[6]

No issue better illustrates the costs that both sides have been willing to incur in support of the special relationship than the allied invasion of Iraq. For Washington, the costs have been primarily in the form of foreign policy adjustments. The George W. Bush administration agreed to reign in its unilateralist instincts for a time and allow its campaign against Saddam Hussein to be tied down in the United Nations (UN) in large part out of respect for the advice and interests of Prime Minister Tony Blair. Conversely, the British Prime Minister was willing to incur severe and foreseeable costs in terms of domestic public opinion and British relations with key European governments when he opted to support the U.S.-led campaign against Iraq. It is very likely that Mr. Blair also understood that by placing the UK in the forefront of the Global War on Terrorism (GWOT), he was increasing the risk that his nation would become the target of retaliation. This very real threat was confirmed on July 7, 2005 (7/7), when coordinated terrorist attacks at four locations in London left 56 people dead and 700 injured.

Both governments accepted these costs and risks because they had gained a new appreciation of the value of the special relationship in the wake of the terrorist attacks of September 11, 2001 (9/11). Indeed, to the extent that there is a silver lining in such catastrophes, it is this tendency to remind us who our friends are and why they deserve our friendship. The specific circumstances of the 9/11 attacks were less important than the shared recognition in Washington and London that the two nations were once again confronting a global threat to the survival of democracy. That shared recognition continues to guide the foreign policy decisions of both governments.

It should come as no surprise that the other nation which has most publicly associated itself with the U.S.-led GWOT is Australia, which shares a cluster of values with Great Britain and the United States. According to James Bennett, values include: ". . . individualism, rule of law, honoring contracts and covenants, and the elevation of freedom to the first rank of political and cultural values."[7] Although these liberal values are prevalent among English-speaking democracies which can trace their roots back to the Magna Carta, they are also celebrated among other nations — including some Central European countries whose leaders developed their world views in opposition to Soviet rule. That these nations have embraced Anglosphere values since the end of the Cold War is testimony both to the enduring validity of these principles and to the international influence of Britain and the United States.

Both the U.S.-UK special relationship and the larger and still protean Anglosphere community have the potential to endure and grow in the 21st century. But both arrangements will require cultivation. Several contributors to this volume have identified areas for improvement in the Anglo-American relationship. First, there is a fair degree of consensus that President Bush must do a much better job of helping Prime Minister Blair to make the case that the GWOT serves the interests of the entire international community. Rhetoric matters in this regard, and the President would be well-advised to carefully study the ways in which Mr. Blair frames his public statements. Perhaps the best example of Mr. Blair's principled eloquence is his first statement following the aforementioned terrorist attacks of 7/7. Speaking from the G8 summit in Gleneagles, Scotland, the Prime Minister noted that all of the participating governments "have some experience of the effects of terrorism and all of the leaders . . . share our complete resolution to defeat this terrorism." He then went on to place the London attacks in a larger context:

> It is particularly barbaric that this has happened on a day when people are meeting to try to help the problems of poverty in Africa and the long term problems of climate change and the environment.[8]

Mr. Blair's statement was more than a tactical device for garnering public support. It demonstrated the Prime Minister's appreciation of Andrew Apostolou's comment that the United States and the UK need to "demonstrate leadership across the spectrum of policy issues, *not* just security."

But rhetoric must also be backed up by actions. The Prime Minister was on fairly safe ground in this regard, since he had committed his nation to a leading role in a 10-year, $25 billion aid initiative for Africa prior to the G8 summit. Mr. Blair has also given a high priority to environmental and climate change issues, as illustrated by the fact that the UK economy grew by 36 percent between 1990 and 2002, while greenhouse gas emissions in the United Kingdom were reduced by 15 percent.[9] It remains to be seen whether the Prime Minister's example will convince President Bush to take a more proactive position on such issues as Third World debt and climate change. Whatever the outcome of these negotiations, however, the two leaders are likely to continue to differ fundamentally in their approaches to issues of international cooperation. Mr. Blair sees international agreements as an indispensable element of British foreign policy, while Mr. Bush is inclined to view them as a trap.

These very different points of view are partly attributable to differences in power. But as Douglas Edlin has observed in his discussion of the positions of the two nations with regard to the International Criminal Court, Great Britain and the United States also draw upon very different historical experiences. Most importantly, there is no counterpart in American history to the British experience of institutionalized cooperation with the North Atlantic Treaty Organization (NATO) and the European Union (EU). Britain has had a mixed record in its efforts to manage this campaign of institutionalized cooperation. The UK has frequently been frustrated in its efforts to play the role of "prefect" to America's "headmaster" within the NATO alliance.[10] Successive British governments also had to overcome intense resistance, both at home and on the continent, before the UK succeeded in joining the European Economic Community (EEC). Furthermore, Great Britain continues to maintain a conditional relationship with the EU. These facts notwithstanding, however, British experiences with NATO and the EU have contributed to the conviction that active participation in international organizations and submission to international laws are essential for the nation's security and prosperity. The challenge for London is to help Washington to realize that it also stands to gain more than it will lose by participating in institutionalized and contractual forms of cooperation with other governments. The two governments will not succeed in convincing the leaders of the world community to actively support the GWOT until the United States sheds its image as the "chief destabilizer" of international order.[11]

The EU poses a special challenge for both the United States and the UK. As John Hulsman accurately predicted during our deliberations, the EU constitution has been rejected by two of the founding members of the European Community. This throws the entire European experiment into confusion and presents both Washington and London with some fundamental choices. For the United States, it will be interpreted by some of President Bush's neo-conservative advisers as an opportunity to press forward with an offensive designed to ensure that the EU will never acquire the capability to pose as an economic or political counterweight to the United States. David Frum and Richard Perle make the case for just such a strategy in their controversial book, *An End to Evil*. The authors recommend that the U.S. "force European governments to choose between Paris and Washington." A key element in their strategy involves prying London away from continental Europe.[12]

Timothy Garton Ash also recommends that the UK abandon its status as the bridge between Washington and Europe, but he argues that Britain should jump in the other direction. He criticizes London for continuing to play the role of Jeeves (the wise but undervalued butler) to a haughty and insensitive Washington long after the benefits of this role have disappeared. Ash concludes that "the British tail will never wag the American dog. Europe, however, is much more than a tail." He calls upon the UK to "change tack" by actively supporting the construction of an EU which is strong enough to say no to the United States and develop its own unique identity in the international system. Charles Dick echoes many of these arguments in his discussion of British defense policy in Chapter 12. The attractions of such a strategy are obvious, particularly at a time when the UK holds the Presidency of the EU. Mr. Ash nonetheless inadvertently highlights one of the major problems with this policy, when he speculates that Great Britain could:

> Give it [the EU] some military muscle. Help it to speak with one voice on major foreign policy issues…[and] find ways of concentrating its large but still diffuse soft power.[13]

Absent some major changes in the ways that leading European governments approach and conduct international relations, British foreign and defense policies are likely to become more constrained, confused, and overextended if they become entangled in the EU's quest for a common foreign policy and a European security and defense identity.

There are two circumstances under which London might feel increasing pressure to choose between Washington and the EU. First, the Bush administration could decide to pursue the divide and conquer strategy recommended by Frum and Perle. Second, certain West European governments could react to the collapse of the EU constitution by attacking London as a "Trojan horse" for U.S. domination and as a bastion of "Anglo-Saxon capitalism." But as Michael Calingaert and others have argued in this volume, it would be extremely difficult for the UK to turn away from the EU, even if the British position within that organization becomes much more uncomfortable. It would also be extremely unwise for London to abandon the special relationship for an unpredictable new relationship with the EU.

Most of the authors in this book would agree that there will probably be no need for the UK to make such a choice for the foreseeable future. Mark Gilbert goes a step further in his chapter, describing the currently fluid transatlantic situation as an opportunity for imaginative statesmanship on the part of both the United States and the United Kingdom. By working together and drawing upon shared institutional, cultural, and political resources, the United States and the UK can expand the opportunities for U.S.-European cooperation, which continues to be an essential precondition for international order and global economic progress.

ENDNOTES - CHAPTER 14

1. Quoted in Douglas Stuart and William Tow, *The Limits of Alliance: NATO Out-Of-Area Problems Since 1949*, Baltimore: Johns Hopkins University Press, 1990, p. 61.

2. *Ibid.*, p. 65.

3. Harold Wilson, *A Personal Record: The Labour Government, 1964-1970*, Boston: Little, Brown, 1971, pp. 39, 187. We can bemoan Wilson's decision to refuse this request as a missed opportunity for high theater, which would have been irresistible to Francis Ford Coppola.

4. Tribute to the Royal Air Force, UK House of Commons, August 20, 1940.

5. Author's interview with Hunt, November 1983.

6. For details regarding the 1962 Nassau Agreement, see Stuart and Tow, *The Limits of Alliance*, pp. 112-121. Critics will be quick to observe, however, that these arrangements served U.S. as well as British interests and occurred only after Washington passed the 1946 McMahon Act, which terminated U.S.-UK nuclear-sharing arrangements.

7. "An Anglosphere Primer," *Foreign Policy Research Institute*, available at *http://www.pattern.com*. See also, Douglas Stuart, "NATO's Anglosphere Option," *International Journal*, Winter, 2004-05, pp. 151-168.

8. A transcript of the Prime Minister's comments is available at *http://www.number-10.gov.uk*.

9. See Blair's important speech on climate change, reproduced at *http://politics.guardian.co.uk/green/story/0,9061,1305030,00.html* . In fairness to Blair's predecessor, the period from 1990 to 1997 was under the Conservative government of John Major.

10. Geoffrey Warner developed this metaphor in "The British Labour Government and the Atlantic Alliance, 1949-1951," in Olav Riste, ed., *Western Security: The Formative Years*, New York: Columbia University Press, 1985, p. 249.

11. The phrase is borrowed from John Gaddis, *Surprise, Security and the American Experience*, Cambridge: Harvard University Press, 2004, p. 101.

12. *An End to Evil: How To Win the War on Terror*, New York: Random House, 2003, pp. 247-250.

13. "No More Jeeves," speech in Brighton, September 30, 2004, reprinted at *http://www.freeworldweb.net*.

ABOUT THE CONTRIBUTORS

ANDREW APOSTOLOU is the Assistant Director of Programs at the Saban Center for Middle East Policy at the Bookings Institution in Washington, D.C. Prior to joining Brookings he served as Vice President, Research, The Foundation for the Defense of Democracies. Formerly, he worked for The Economist Group's Economist Intelligence Unit (EIC), covering the former Soviet Union. His doctoral research at St. Antony's College, Oxford, deals with his topic, "Bystanders and Collaborators during the Holocaust in Northern Greece." Mr. Apostolou was a freelance researcher on Central Asia and the Middle East for the Royal Institute of International Affairs. He has worked as a consultant on the Middle East, specializing in Saudi Arabia. He has given many lectures and presentations to numerous colleges and corporations as well as serving as a consultant and interviewee for various topics for various TV/radio outlets such as Fox (O'Reilly Factor, Fox and Friends, Your World with Neil Cavuto), as well as CNN, CNN International, CNBC, and the BBC domestic television and radio, to name a few. Mr. Apostolou received his master's degree from the London School of Economics (Logic & Scientific Method).

MICHAEL CALINGAERT is the Executive Vice President, Council for the United States and Italy. The Council is based at the Brookings Institution, where he continues his academic/research activities as a Visiting Scholar at the Center on the United States and Europe. He is a member of the Political Section, Institute of European Studies, Free University of Brussels. Mr. Calingaert's previous positions include director of European Operations for the Pharmaceutical Manufacturers Association; Economic and Commercial Minister at the U.S. Embassy, London; Deputy Assistant Secretary for International Resources and Food Policy at the U.S. Department of State; and Economic Minister at the U.S. Embassy, Rome. Mr. Calingaert wrote *The 1992 Challenge from Europe: Development of the European Community's Internal Market*, the first U.S. study of the European community's single market. His most recent book, *European Integration Revisited: Progress, Prospects and U.S. Interest*, was published in 1996. He has also written various articles on European developments for *Business Economics, California Management Review*, and the *New York Times*, to mention a few. Mr. Calingaert graduated from Swarthmore College (history) and pursued graduate studies at the University of Cologne (history and politics), and at the University of California in Berkeley (economics).

NICHOLAS CHILDS is the BBC Pentagon Correspondent. He joined the BBC in 1982, with extensive previous experience reporting on the armed forces of various countries. He has worked as BBC World Affairs Correspondent, reporter for BBC World TV, Defense and British Affairs Analyst for BBC World Service radio, and briefly as reporter for *Jane's Defence Weekly* magazine, as well as contributing to various journals on defense and international relations issues. Mr. Childs specializes in the Middle East, reporting on Israel and the Palestinians, Afghanistan, the Balkans, Sierra Leone, and Iraq. As a BBC reporter, he covered the Iran-Iraq War, the Iraqi invasion of Kuwait, and Operation DESERT STORM. Mr. Childs holds a master's degree in Modern History and Economics from St. Catherine's College, Oxford.

CHARLES DICK is a historian by training and an intelligence officer by profession. He served as an associate of the Soviet Studies Research Center (SSRC) and in 1989 became the director of the SSRC, now renamed the Conflicts Studies Research Centre. He served as a director in the UK Higher Command and Staff Course theater war game and now acts in a similar capacity for the Allied Rapid Reaction Corps. He also worked as a special consultant to the Ministry of Defence. Mr. Dick has published extensively in the *Royal United Services' Institute Journal, International Defense Review, Military Review, Jane's Intelligence Review,* and the *Journal of Slavic Military Studies,* for which he serves as assistant editor. In addition, he has authored numerous manuals, operations and tactics documents, and threat assessments on defense issues. In 1966, Mr. Dick completed a manual on general enemy (*Genforce*) which was adopted by NATO.

DOUGLAS E. EDLIN is an Assistant Professor of Political Science at Dickinson College. His research concentrates on the Anglo-American common law tradition, the development of judicial review in the United States, and the legal and policy issues surrounding the use and regulation of assisted reproductive technology. Professor Edlin is editing a collection of essays on the common law tradition and has written on the development of extra-constitutional judicial review in the United States, the ambiguity precondition in British constitutional theory, and the legal paradigms employed by American courts when resolving disputes about frozen embryos. Recent publications include *From Ambiguity to Legality: The Future of English Judicial Review, Rule Britannia,* and *Common Law Theory* (Cambridge University Press, forthcoming) Professor Edlin holds a Ph.D. from Oxford University and a J.D. from Cornell Law School.

NILE GARDINER is Fellow in Anglo-American Security Policy at the Douglas and Sarah Allison Center for Foreign Policy Studies, Heritage Foundation, in Washington. His key areas of specialization include the Anglo-U.S. Special Relationship, the United Nations, postwar Iraq, and the role of Great Britain and Europe in the U.S.-led alliance against international terrorism and "rogue states." As a leading authority on transatlantic relations, Dr. Gardiner has advised the Executive Branch of the United States Government on a range of key issues, from the role of international allies in postwar Iraq, to U.S.-British leadership in the war on terror. Prior to joining Heritage, he was Foreign Policy Researcher for former British Prime Minister Margaret Thatcher. Dr. Gardiner received his Ph.D. in History from Yale University in 1998.

MARK GILBERT is an Associate Professor of Contemporary European History, University of Trento, Italy, and was Professorial Lecturer, Johns Hopkins School for Advanced International Studies, Spring 2000 and Spring 2005. He served as Assistant Professor of Political Science at Dickinson College in Pennsylvania, 1993-96, and lecturer in European Studies at the University of Bath from 1997 to 2002. Dr. Gilbert's areas of expertise include the history of European integration post-1945, European and transatlantic history, and contemporary Italian political history. His published works include *The Italian Revolution: The End of Politics Italian Style? The Lega Nord and the Northern Question in Italian Politics*, and *Surpassing Realism: The Politics of European Integration since 1945*, as well as numerous articles in professional journals such as the *Journal of Contemporary History, Political Quarterly, Journal of Modern Italian Studies, Government & Opposition, Modern Italy*, and *World Policy Journal*. Dr. Gilbert earned his B.A. with honors in Politics from the University of Durham and his Ph.D. from the University of Wales.

JOHN C. HULSMAN is Senior Research Fellow at the Heritage Foundation. He concentrates on European security and NATO affairs, the European Union, U.S.-European trade and economic relations, and the war on terror. He is also a frequent commentator on all aspects of transatlantic relations, global geopolitics, and international cooperation in fighting terrorism. Dr. Hulsman makes regular appearances with major media outlets such as ABC, Fox News, CNN, MSNBC, PBS, and the BBC. Prior to assuming his current position, he was a fellow in European studies at the Center for Strategic and International Studies (CSIS). He also taught world politics and U.S. foreign policy at the University of St. Andrews, Scotland, where he specialized in American foreign policy during the post-Cold War era, and the relationship between NATO and the European Union.

JEFFREY D. MCCAUSLAND is the Director of the Leadership in Conflict Initiative at Dickinson College and special consultant to CBS News. Dr. McCausland has served as Director for Defense Policy and Arms Control on the National Security Council and also held research positions at the IISS (London), the Center for International Affairs (Harvard University), and the Marshall Center (Germany). Following retirement from the position of Dean of Academics at the U.S. Army War College, he accepted a chair in Leadership at the U.S. Naval Academy (Annapolis). He has written extensively on U.S. defense affairs and international security.

LEO MICHEL is a Senior Research Fellow at the Institute for National Strategic Studies, concentrating on transatlantic security issues. Formerly, he was director for NATO Policy within the Office of the Secretary of Defense (OSD). He was responsible for policy formulation, support, and advice to the Secretary and other senior Defense officials on NATO defense and capabilities planning, NATO's role in war on terrorism, NATO-led operations in Bosnia (SFOR), Kosovo (KFOR), NATO enlargement, NATO relations with the European Union, Partnership for Peace, and NATO-Russia and NATO-Ukraine relations.

ERIK R. PETERSON is the William A. Schreyer Chair in Global Analysis, Director, Seven Revolutions Initiative, and Senior VP at CSIS. He was formerly the director of research at Kissinger Associates. He is a Fellow of the World Economic Forum, a board member of the Center for Global Business Studies at Penn State University, a member of the Advisory Board of the Global Capital Markets Center at Duke University, and a member of the Advisory Board of the Center for the Study of the Presidency. Mr. Peterson holds an MBA in international finance from the Wharton School at the University of Pennsylvania, and an M.A. in international law and economics from the School of Advanced International Studies at Johns Hopkins University. He also holds the Certificate of Eastern European Studies from the University of Fribourg in Switzerland and the Certificate in International Legal Studies from the Hague Academy of International Law in the Netherlands.

RAY RAYMOND, MBE, FRSA, is the Political Officer, British Consul-General, in New York. He has spent much of his professional career facilitating political, financial, and academic dialogue between the United States and Great Britain. Dr. Raymond is a expert on both British and American diplomatic history and has lectured on the Special Relationship at Columbia University.

MITCHELL B. REISS is Vice Provost for International Affairs and Professor of Law and Professor of Government at the College of William and Mary, where he joined the faculty in 1999. Previously he practiced law at Covington & Burling in Washington, DC; served as Former Assistant Director and Senior Policy Advisor of the Korean Peninsula Energy Development Organization; was Guest Scholar at the Woodrow Wilson International Center for Scholars; and former White House Fellow serving as special assistant to the National Security Council. Dean Reiss was on a leave of absence from the Law School and the College from August 2003 to February 2005. He served as Director of the Office of Policy Planning at the U.S. Department of State from July 2003 to February 2005. He was appointed in January 2004 by President George W. Bush as Special Envoy to the Northern Ireland Peace Process with the rank of Ambassador, a position he currently holds. He is the author of *Bridled Ambition: Why Countries Constrain Their Nuclear Capabilities* and *Without the Bomb: The Politics of Nuclear Non-proliferation;* co-editor and author of *The Nuclear Tipping Point* and *Nuclear Proliferation after the Cold War;* and has published numerous articles in leading journals and newspapers in the United States, Europe, and Asia. He holds a J.D. from Columbia University; a D.Phil. from Oxford University; an M.A.L.D. from the Fletcher School, and a B.A. from Williams College.

PHILIP STEPHENS has been the Associate Editor and Senior Commentator of the *Financial Times* since 1983. He is a well-known author, commentator, and broadcaster. Before joining the *Financial Times,* he was a correspondent for *Reuters* in London and Brussels. Mr. Stephens is the author of *Politics and the Pound,* a study of the British Government's exchange rate management and its relations with Europe since 1979; and *Tony Blair, a* biography of the British Prime Minister. He is a Fulbright Fellow and winner of the 2002 David Watt Prize for Outstanding Political Journalism. Mr. Stephens was educated at Wimbledon College and at Oxford University, where he took an honors degree in modern history.

DOUGLAS T. STUART is the first holder of the J. William and Helen D. Stuart Chair in International Studies at Dickinson College. He is also an Adjunct Professor at the U.S. Army War College. Professor Stuart is the author or editor of seven books, three monographs, and over 30 published articles relating to U.S. national security policy, NATO politics, and Asia-Pacific security. He is a former NATO Fellow and a guest scholar at the Brookings Institution, the U.S. State Department, and the Elliott School of George Washington University. Professor Stuart received his Ph.D. in International Relations from the University of Southern California. He is a recipient of both the Ganoe Prize for Inspirational Teaching and the Distinguished Teaching Award at Dickinson College.